The Power and Perception of Dreams

Wakefulness and the dream state go hand in hand, equal halves of our existence in this three-dimensional world. *The Psychic Side of Dreams* points out the real nature of the dream state, and the four basic forms of dreaming—analyzing for the first time what until now had been considered one single state of consciousness exhibiting several different aspects.

Supported by numerous case histories from people in many walks of life and locations, *The Psychic Side of Dreams* deals authoritatively with the four types of dreams, namely dreams due to illness or physical or mental stress; dreams indicating suppressed emotional problems (the very dreams psycho-analysis thrives on); out-of-the-body experiences, which is really not dreaming at all, but to many subjects, feels like dreaming, at least at first and until fully understood; and psychic dreams, which are channels of communication between another dimension and ours containing such material as predictions, other forms of psychic information, and warnings, to be heeded to avoid problems.

This, then, may be the definitive book on dreams, explaining what they are, and what they mean. The book is the result of many years of research and direct investigations by Prof. Hans Holzer. *The Psychic Side of Dreams* will open up the reader's understanding of his or her own hidden powers and perceptive abilities.

D1358561

FATE Presents. . .

THE PSYCHIC SIDE OF DREAMS

HANS HOLZER

1994
Llewellyn Publications
St. Paul, Minnesota 55164-0383, U.S.A.

"What Exactly Is a Dream?," "Prophetic Dreams" & "Reincarnation Dreams" also appear in *ESP, Witches & UFOs: The Best of Hans Holzer, Book II* (Llewellyn Publications, 1991).

Cover art by Suzanne DeVeuve

previously printed hardcover by Doubleday 1973

FIRST LLEWELLYN EDITION 1992
Second Printing 1994

Library of Congress Cataloging-in-Publication Data

Holzer, Hans
      The psychic side of dreams / by Hans Holzer
        p.   cm. — (Fate presents)
      Includes bibliographical references.
      ISBN 0-87542-369-8
      1. Dreams 2. Parapsychology. I. Title. II. Series.
BF1078.H67 1992   91-24523
135′ .3—dc20   CIP

Llewellyn Publications
A Division of Llewellyn Worldwide, Ltd.
P.O. Box 64383, St. Paul, MN 55164-0383

About the FATE Presents Series

Since 1948, FATE magazine has brought to readers around the world true, documented reports of the strange and unusual. For over four decades FATE has reported on such subjects as UFOs and space aliens, Bigfoot, the Loch Ness monster, ESP, psychic powers, divination, ghosts and poltergeists, startling new scientific theories and breakthroughs, real magic, near-death and out-of-body experiences, survival after death, Witches and Witchcraft and many other topics that will even astound your imagination.

FATE has revealed the fakers and the frauds and examined the events and people with powers that defy explanation. If you read it in FATE, the information was certified and factual.

One of the things that makes FATE special is the wide variety of authors who write for it. Some of them have numerous books to their credit and are highly respected in their fields of specialty. Others are plain folks—like you and me—whose lives have crossed over into the world of the paranormal.

Now we are publishing a series of books bearing the FATE name. You hold one such book in your hands. The topic of this book may be one of any of the subjects we've described or a variety of them. It may be a collection of authenticated articles by unknown writers or a book by an author of world-renown.

There is one thing of which you can be assured: the occurrences described in this book are absolutely accurate and took place as noted. Now even more people will be able to marvel at, be shocked by and enjoy *true reports of the strange and unusual.*

Other Books by Hans Holzer

Available from Llewellyn:

CONTENTS

To Morpheus and his fascinating companions,
Fama and Persephone

INTRODUCTION

There are at least half a dozen popular songs registered at the copyright office under the title "Dream." Next to romantic developments, there is possibly no single subject that occupies the mind of the average person more than the subject of dreams. Dreaming is not something a chosen few do or care to discuss, it happens to everyone without exception. It is a subject always fit for discussion no matter what the circumstances. Like eating and sleeping, dreaming affects everyone. Nor is it something new that has just popped up on the horizon; on the contrary, preoccupation with dreams and their meanings goes back to the very beginnings of humankind. It is therefore not surprising to find an enormous number of misconceptions about dreams—misconceptions that have been perpetuated from generation to generation, regardless of social or economic circumstances or nationality.

Ever since humans discovered that they dream, they have wanted to know why, how and what it meant in relation to their waking existence. At the beginning of their development these questions were answered by the shaman or the priest of a particular society. As humans became more sophisticated, they consulted medical practitioners about their dreams, at the same time retaining the religious consultant as a secondary source of possible information. When neither the medical nor the religious expert sufficed and the quest for a better understanding of dreams continued, they turned to occult sources for definitions and explanations. So we have from a very early time onward the hidden meanings of dreams—meanings that can only be explained and interpreted by those familiar with the language of occultism.

With the onset of the so-called scientific age, heralded by nineteenth-century materialism, dreams became taboo in the sense that the scientifically oriented human should have no recourse to such seemingly meaningless information. For almost a century, those who considered themselves sophisticated would not own up publicly to the belief in or study of dreams, out of fear of being ridiculed or held in contempt in an age that strove for materialistic gains and technical accomplishments. For a while, then, the significance of dreams was relegated to primitive members of society, to the very young or the very old, the superstitious, and the misinformed. It remained for Dr. Sigmund Freud of Vienna to rekindle interest in dream material, and once again the subject of dreams became of paramount importance.

At first, psychoanalysis met with hostility on the part of conventional medical practitioners as well as the general public. For Freud and his disciples were convinced that all dreams contained sexual symbols and that sexual maladjustment lay at the bottom of human problems. It seemed absurd that significant deductions could be obtained from dream material—even more absurd, nay, even shocking, to see such suppressed sexual dreams as Dr. Freud indicated.

But Freud prevailed in the end, and the turn of the twentieth century saw increasing acceptance of his new ideas concerning the nature of humankind and especially the significance of dreams. From nearly a century of too little attention to dreams, and a total disbelief in their importance in the understanding of human nature, humankind now turned the other way—everything could be explained through dreams, all problems, no matter how complex, could be significantly understood through the study of a subject's dreams.

Over the years, the more progressive thinkers readily accepted the theories of Freud and his successors. But the common people, especially those who could never afford psychoanalysis for economic reasons or those who would not accept it on religious grounds, found themselves suddenly cut off from an element that had supplied a great deal of encouragement in their otherwise drab lives. The hope for a better future as expressed in dreams was relegated to popular superstition by the nineteenth century, even though it continued to be of interest. Now medical science had resurrected this material and made it its own, albeit with totally new and, to many simple people, unacceptable interpretations. These people could not see any sexual significance in their dreams, yet they knew they were dreaming all the time. Without an official channel to turn to, they went to occult practitioners for their dream interpretations, many times practitioners who claimed occult knowledge while frequently possessing none. A rash of Gypsy dream books, written by individuals with very little learning, appeared. What truth there was in these books was mainly derived from ancient sources, symbolic in nature, and very difficult to understand by those not fully cognizant of the deeply rooted symbolism of occult interpretations of dreams. In order to curry favor with the masses, however, these popular dream books needed to express their counsel in practical and simple terms. As a result, we have "Babylonian" dream books listing all kinds of possible dream situations and blissfully converting them into numbers to be gambled on at the local betting counter. For those among the readers who didn't care to bet, there was always a handy interpretation of certain dreams. Since these meanings contained a number of variations widely differing in significance, nearly every interpretation fitted. The reader simply selected the one most suited to his/her situation and as a result did his/her own interpreting. Needless to add, dream books of this kind, with rare exceptions, had no evidential value whatsoever. But they served a psychological purpose, in continuing an ancient tradition as to the significance of dreams in human lives, and they helped people in need of such crutches to continue their frequently unhappy existence, always hoping that a dream would reveal a better and possibly a richer future. As I will show later, a significant number of dreams contain material of a psychic nature—material that later becomes objective reality in the lives of those who dream it. This is common knowledge, not only among those who have studied these subjects but among untrained people as well. The fact that many people dream "true," the fact that one never knows who is thus gifted, was and is a powerful incentive for people to carry on, no matter how difficult their present circumstances may be.

Finally, the inevitable had to happen: Freudian interpretation of dreams was seriously challenged by other analysts, notably the followers of Carl Jung. The purely sexual interpretation of the symbolism in dreams gave way to a combination of other factors, particularly material pertaining to environmental pressures, early experiences of a non-sexual nature, individual characteristics of personality, and eventually even to psychic elements. More and more psychoanalysts are looking toward the occult sciences with a respectful eye, and some have even included occult material in their interpretations and investigations.

With the more general acceptance of psychoanalysis as seen through the eyes of Carl

Jung, Karen Horney and other middle-of-the-road practitioners, dreams were no longer the exclusive vehicle of the psychoanalyst. Once again, dream material was available to other investigators to see whether some of it did not account for the phenomena with which parapsychology is concerned. In the 1930s, Professor Joseph Banks Rhine established the first American parapsychology laboratory at Duke University in Durham, North Carolina, and from that moment on, dream material became a very substantial and important component of all psychical research.

The present book has been written not to explain conventional dreams by one of several possible psychiatric or psychoanalytical theories, nor as a metaphysical compendium to interpret the frequently obtuse meaning found in dreams. My purpose is to establish as clearly as possible the nature of sleep, without which dreams would have no existence, the many aspects of dreaming, and how dreams fit into the complex triune of body-mind-spirit which we call human personality. Far too much double talk has been published on the subject of dreams already; neither mystical verbiage that really doesn't say anything specific, nor medical categorizing will help the individual understand his/her dreams. To the contrary, such works only tend to confuse. I have therefore tried to set down, in as simple and popular language as I am capable of, the various aspects of dreams and subdivisions as I see them, and I have supported my contentions with large selections of significant material from my files—material that has been thoroughly researched and verified. I want to establish the great importance dreams have for our lives, on all levels, and to help individuals in all walks of life cope with their dreams in a useful and constructive manner.

My point of view is one of objectivity, as objective, anyway, as any human being can be. I am not beholden to any particular religious interpretation of dreams. I have no hang-ups about them, nor do I accept the findings of any scientist in any field as final. Learning is a continuing process and it may well be that in the years to come I, along with others, will learn new facts and facets of dream interpretation not now known. But at present I have before me the results of fifteen years of research in the field, a considerable amount of case material, and my accumulated experience through hypnotherapy of cases that have been referred to me by medical doctors.

I hope this book will prove of practical and immediate value to those reading it, and help other researchers enter new avenues of inquiry into human personality, taking into account all elements germane to that triune which we are, and excluding nothing that may be of evidential value, even if it should pertain to a dimension other than the common physical one with which we are most familiar. Only by looking at humankind as a whole entity can we learn the truth.

—Prof. Hans Holzer, Ph.D.

THE NATURE OF SLEEP

Before we can discuss dreams we must fully understand the nature of their companion, sleep, without which dreaming would have no objective reality. If humans were only living organisms consisting of certain chemical combinations, without a non-physical component called spirit or soul, then they would simply rest for certain periods of time in order to recharge their batteries of energy. In that case, sleep would be simply the absence of consciousness, and would result in a total disconnection of all ongoing activities within the body. That's not the case, however: we know very well that certain vital functions continue during sleep, even if at reduced levels, and that, in fact, sleep is by no means a total disconnection from activities as is shutting off a machine. So the materialistic concept of humankind, as it was popular in the nineteenth century, is without validity and its position in the universe is by no means similar to that of a manmade machine, but something far more complex. The need for sleep arises from the expenditure of physical or mental energy. Either of these expenditures may induce fatigue, not an unnatural state but rather the result of "built in" activity cycles. When the energy potential runs down, the human machine stops, and sleep results. After sleep has been completed, the human machine continues to function. During sleep the conscious mind rests temporarily, while the unconscious part of the mind continues to function. Vital activities of the bodily machine are carried on automatically, in order to preserve the organism. The temporary exclusion of the conscious mind allows the body and the unconscious mind to regain spent energies from the reservoir represented by the human energy field that is located within the confines of the physical body.

Human personality consists of an electro-magnetic field containing a certain power potential which is encased in an outer layer of dense matter called the physical body. This field, also known as the *aura*, is unique with every human being and contains varying amounts of energy. Reaching slightly beyond the physical skin, its outer limits can frequently be observed by those who are sensitive enough to see it. The inner body itself is the astral or etheric body referred to by psychical researchers. It is this inner body that is the seat of personality, memory, emotions and all that which makes up a human being, while the outer layer, or physical body, does not possess powers of its own without directions from the inner body. This is at variance with nineteenth-century materialism, of course, but more and more researchers are becoming aware of the existence of this secondary body. (There have been published accounts of a "bioplasmic" body that is responsible for the occurrence of psychic phenomena, including psychokinesis, or the movement of objects by thought power.)

This arrangement seems quite logical; when we disconnect the user of energy from the reservoir, we allow the "back-up crew" to stock up on fresh energy, so the user can have it when he/she returns to consciousness. Perhaps the following comparison will be easier to understand: you had a certain amount of money in the bank, and you have spent it all. You know that a payment is due you regularly every other week, so you curtail your spending for a few days until the next payment comes in. As soon as the new payment is in the bank, you are notified that you have money in your account, and you can spend once again. This is how sleep restores the power reservoir of the human body. Since the amount of sleep required by individuals varies greatly according to personalities, conditions, health factors, age, even social and economic situations, it is difficult to say just how much sleep a human being needs. From my own observations I have come to the conclusion that the amount of sleep depends on the state of the power reservoir, the need to restore spent energies, which may differ not only with various individuals but with the same individual depending upon circumstances. It seems to me that sleep is the amount of time required for a particular individual to restore his/her power reservoir to maximum efficiency, to that level the power reservoir had when the individual came into this life. I am also convinced that the newborn baby already contains the seed of his/her eventual power reservoir even if the full extent of that reservoir is not reached until some years later. The amount of this life-force differs from person to person, and sleep restores the power reservoir only to that extent. Even if a person were to sleep enormous amounts of time in order to strengthen the power reservoir, he/she would not be able to accumulate more than he/she had originally. This is so because each individual's power reservoir capacity was set at birth and, once filled, excess energies restored through long hours of sleep would simply drop off, as it were, and find no storage capabilities within his/her system.

Unfortunately, many individuals suffer from insomnia or irregular sleeping habits. The desired sleeping period, whether it is six, seven, eight, nine or even ten hours, should be consummated in one stretch. Occasionally, this is not possible for a number of reasons: these may be health problems, unresolved emotional problems, environmental discomforts, noises, lack of air, lack of proper sleeping surfaces, or other external factors. Regardless of what causes the irregular sleeping patterns, the approach in dealing with them should take into account the need to establish uninterrupted sleeping habits, if possible. The less the restorative cycle is interrupted or weakened, the better for the organism. Short sleeping periods never equal the total of one long period spent asleep. The continuity of sleep is of paramount importance.

In dealing with insomnia, it is important to establish what factors cause interrupted sleep. Once the reasons have been isolated, they should be written down. Then a list of potential remedies should be put next to the causative factors. Reading this "prescription" to oneself, preferably aloud, and determining what one will do the following day to remedy the problems is the first step toward resumption of uninterrupted sleep. While the removal of the unresolved problems is of great importance, the second step is equally as vital in restoring or preserving uninterrupted sleep. This is the "light suggestion" that sleep should come at such and such a time, without the pressure of concentration or any kind of forceful order. The stronger the command, the less it is likely to be obeyed by the unconscious, which controls the sleep pattern.

Once the suggestion has been made to go to sleep at a certain time, the clock should be visualized with the hands pointing at the particular time desired for the dropping off to sleep. Then the subject must be changed immediately, and not dwelt upon. At the appointed moment, the unconscious will nudge the mind to give the proper command to the sleep center in the brain, and sleep should ensue. Reliance upon chemical agents is not advised; they may work faster at first, but eventually lose their effectiveness, resulting in a backlash of anxiety. I have frequently heard people say the the body will fall asleep when it is tired enough; that is not entirely true, because unresolved emotional factors can prevent the body from exercising its natural functions.

A third element of importance in the restoration of uninterrupted sleep is the realization that an individual's sleeping period is in tune with his/her natural pattern. A diurnal person should not attempt to do night work and a nocturnal individual should not force him/herself to rise early in the morning. Going against one's own nature is never warranted, despite such poetic dicta as "The early bird gets the worm."

Death has frequently been referred to as eternal sleep. This, of course, is based upon religious concepts under which humans die and "sleep" in their graves until such time as they are resurrected and called before the throne of God for judgment. This is not merely a Christian concept but exists also in the Egyptian religion, where the soul of the dead is judged by Thoth. The considerable resemblance between sleep and death is at the base of such concepts; primitive humans observed that a dead person seemed asleep, at least on the surface. Somehow the idea that the body of the deceased was sleeping for all eternity seemed more acceptable than the more realistic concept that the physical body was rapidly deteriorating after it was put underground, where it was unable to sustain life without a directing force of spirit. Organized religion took up this natural euphemism by incorporating it into its doctrine of reward for the just and punishment for the wicked. Thus resurrection comes as the ultimate reward, although a specific time for it is not set. But the belief in a resurrection of the physical body as prevalent in the Roman Catholic faith is a variance with observed nature; primitive humans, seeing that everything around them came back in the spring, were far more inclined to accept reincarnation as a principle in nature than the restoration of what in their hearts they knew could not be restored. In order to accept the physical restoration they needed to accept a possible miracle, which in turn required the all-powerful presence of a discerning deity. All this was part and parcel of a political church and a structure more designed to keep the faithful in line than to present a realistic picture of the hereafter.

But the similarity between sleep and death is superficial. In sleep, all vital functions are retained, and bodily movement continues. In death all vital functions cease, and the body is lifeless. Nevertheless, the euphemism continues. We speak of "putting an animal to sleep" when we really mean kill it. Our cemeteries are dotted with sorrowful expressions of bereavement, wishing our dear departed ones a peaceful sleep. We tell each other that so-and-so has gone on to eternal rest, when we have no proof whatever that he/she has done so.

From the very beginning of humankind, the sleep portion of human existence was also a time when unusual manifestations could take place.

These would occur more often in the dream state, which lies within the sleep condition. But they could also occur when the individual was merely asleep and not yet dreaming. I am speaking here of revelations occurring to the sleeper, revelations which are not caused by external entities but by the individual him/herself. In the sleep state, when the conscious mind is temporarily shut off, the unconscious is capable of delivering to the upper strata of the mind certain messages which the individual is incapable of grasping in the wakeful state. Thus sleep is a time for inspiration, a time to draw on inner resources not usually available to the individual in his/her state of wakefulness. There are countless instances of visits by the deity or celestials to human beings while they are asleep. Of course, a conventional psychoanalyst might say that these Biblical characters simply *dreamt* that God or an angel had visited them, and upon awakening, had recorded their vivid dreams.

After studying many hundreds of cases involving seeming psychic communications from the world beyond, however, I find that there is a marked difference between a dream communication with superior beings, and an actual "visitation" by such entities. The descriptive pattern differs; when we are dealing with a psychic dream, it is in the form of a *message* and, in the material in my possession at least, these messages stem from human beings, even if on the Other Side of life. On the other hand, the Biblical and other religious visitors represent more of a close and immediate presence, physically present with the sleeper, who does not see or hear them with his/her ordinary senses but with the unconscious mind operating *through* the ordinary senses at a much reduced level of activity. Thus the individual does not awake while the celestial visitor is with him/her, but he/she hears every word, perceives with closed eyes, and remembers what was said or shown to him/her upon awakening. Sleep, especially by individuals known for their pious leanings, was considered almost sacred in many cultures, and prophecies and pronouncements of a profound nature frequently followed periods of sleep in which the individual would open him/herself up to contact by superior forces.

Frequently, healing takes place during sleep. This does not cover only psychic healing, presumably under the influence of an external individual, but ordinary healing as well. The medical profession has long prescribed periods of sleep for recuperative purposes. This is done not because the doctor wants the patient out of his/her hair, and hopes that periods of sleep will provide respite from the patient's demands, but because real recuperation occurs in the sleep state, when energies can be freed to perform the job of restoring the body to full harmony. Thus the prescription of rest for a sick person is by no means a palliative, but a form of positive, active therapy. It should be noted here, however, that dreaming takes some, though not many, energies away from the recuperative processes. And some periods of sleep without some dreaming are rare.

Sexual relationships in most societies take place at night, either prior to or during the sleep period, or upon awakening from it. In fact, the euphemism for having sexual intercourse is "sleeping with someone" in most languages. The reason for this prevailing pattern is by no means the need for darkness for this closest of all human relations. Some of the most pleasurable sex takes place in full daylight or under subdued light conditions; while people about to go to sleep are generally tired from the day's work and not likely to have too many energies left for sexual intercourse. So the reasons why nighttime sleep has been connected with sex from time immemorial must be found elsewhere. Could it not be that the recuperative element in sleep is directly tied to the expenditure of energies during sexual intercourse? Whether the relationship occurs prior to sleep, with sleep restoring energies spent, or whether it occurs during sleep or early in the morning, using freshly restored energies, the link between sex and sleep seems at once obvious and natural. Sexual relations are, of course, also a powerful sleep-inducing factor because they bring about overall relaxation of tension and thus facilitate the gliding into the sleep state.

Natural sleep is not the only way by which the sleep state can be obtained. Hypnotic sleep is an artificial form of inducing the sleep state, using the power of suggestion and exclusion—the environment, external noises or stimuli and the restriction of perception to the voice of the hypnotist. Hypnosis works only if the subject desires it; success in hypnotically induced sleep depends 90 per cent upon the subject and 10 per cent upon the operator. Even the slightest doubt or block in the mind of the subject will make hypnotic sleep impossible. There are a number of basic differences between natural sleep and hypnotically induced sleep. For one thing, hypnotic sleep can be produced in an individual even if the person is fully rested, in fact, immediately following a night's sleep. Since the sleep state is suggested, the actual condition of the person's body and mind does not prevent it from occurring. The hypnotist creates conditions conducive to the sleep state and suggests to the subject that they are real. If the bond between subject and hypnotist is good and strong, the subject will accept the hypnotist's suggestions as reality and obey them. On awakening from hypnotically induced sleep, most subjects feel extremely relaxed, especially if a suggestion to that effect has been implanted prior to awakening. But in addition, good subjects also feel a sense of continuity with what occurred just prior to hypnosis taking place. Frequently they have a loss of time, and are unable to remember what transpired during the period of hypnotic sleep. This is frequently necessary, especially with hypnotherapy, since the hypnotist wants to eliminate certain negative factors from the unconscious of the subject. Although hypnotic sleep can be manipulated in precisely the same way natural sleep occurs, allowing the body to restore its energy batteries, this need not necessarily be the case.

In hypnosis, there are three levels of depth, and only the third, or deepest, level approximates natural sleep. In this condition the hypnotist can implant suggestions or eliminate unwanted material from the unconscious mind of the subject. This is of course impossible with natural sleep. Suggestions made to a sleeper, whether at night or in the daytime, will go unheard unless the sleeper awakens. Not so with hypnotic sleep, where every word spoken by the hypnotist is of importance and impact. Post-hypnotic suggestions frequently form part of the pattern of hypnosis. This is also impossible with ordinary sleep. In recent years some devices have been developed which suggest the possibility of learning while you sleep. These are primarily low-level recording devices which contain suggestions to be implanted into the unconscious mind of the sleeper. But as the sleeper has not been hypnotically treated, the authority of the hypnotist is absent, and consequently the effectiveness of such devices is questionable.

Hypnosis can be a valuable aid in two conditions closely related to dreaming and sleeping. With individuals who have difficulties maintaining regular sleeping habits hypnotic suggestion may indeed remove blocks and suggest certain sleeping patterns. In this case the use of post-hypnotic suggestion leads an individual to the sleep state when it is desired. Only trained hypnotists should undertake such procedures, however, as their effectiveness and indeed their safety depend upon exact timing and wording of commands. It should only be applied to individuals without psychosomatic or psychoneurotic problems, or under the supervision of a trained physician familiar with hypnotic techniques.

The second use for hypnosis in connection with the dream state is the ability of the hypnotist to recall forgotten dreams from the unconscious mind of the subject. This can be of great importance with deeply buried psychoanalytical material, in conditions involving anxiety, or in research dealing with reincarnation material which is not consciously remembered but which may, nevertheless, be ferreted out and brought to the surface by hypnotic means, in order to be analyzed and its significance related to the current mental and physical condition of the subject. The latter use of hypnosis should only be undertaken by physicians familiar with parapsychological concepts or by parapsychologists aware of the proper precautions to be taken with neurotic individuals.

Humans are not the only living things restoring energies through sleep. Animals do the same; and I am convinced that animals also dream. Unfortunately, we are blocked from learning the details of such material except at times in a secondary fashion from their abnormal behavior as the result of anxiety dreams. Even in the case of plants a state simulating human and animal sleep exists, when the plant's functions seem to be greatly restricted for periods of time. I am convinced that plants restore their energy potentials in precisely the same way humans and animals do, since they share with the higher order of living beings the inner, or astral, body contained within a physical, three-dimensional shell.

WHAT EXACTLY IS
A DREAM?

Even some pretty well educated people frequently do not know the difference between sleep and dream, that is, they are not cognizant of the fact that certain processes occur during the sleep stage while others occur only while an individual is dreaming. This is of course understandable since sleep and dream come together, as it were, occupying the same period in the time continuum. But they are not identical—to sleep does not necessarily mean to dream, and there are states of dreaming that are not truly part of the sleep state, in which a person can come pretty close to being awake though not fully conscious. The majority of dreams, however, certainly occur while a person is asleep. In fact, I would prefer to say one is either asleep or awake, and one can be asleep and "adream" at the same time. Of course, not remembering a dream does not mean that a dream, or dreams, has not occurred. Individual observation of the dream state, while it is the primary source of content, is nevertheless not reliable in an objective way. The dream memory fades quickly upon awakening and the sleeper may simply not remember. Although some materialistically inclined people tend to dismiss dreaming as the equivalent of fantasizing, this was not always so. Prior to nineteenth-century materialism, dreaming was considered serious business. William Shakespeare frequently refers to the dream state as a state of great significance. "To sleep: perchance to dream ... " (*Hamlet*) and "We are such stuff as dreams are made on" (*The Tempest*) are two of the better-known quotations which indicate how important Shakespeare and his contemporaries found dream material to be to the creative and intellectual processes in humans.

What exactly happens to body, mind and spirit when we are asleep? How do dreams come into being? According to Sandra Shulman, English writer on comparative religion, oneirology, or the study and interpretation of dreams, was originally associated and inseparably tied in with the mystic roots of civilization, religion and magic, to which medicine was also closely tied. She says, "Dreams might have remained in the nebulous atmosphere of poetry, superstition, and fairground quackery, but at the end of the last century a Viennese doctor, Sigmund Freud, saw them as the keys with which to unlock the doors of man's unconscious."

But what hath Freud wrought? Nothing less than the total rejection by establishment scientists and those following them of the ancient wisdoms contained in pre-Freud dream interpretation, nothing less than the rejection of the psychic elements contained in the dream material and all the other manifestations of an external derivation which did not fit in with Freud's notion of dreams representing the suppressed libido. One of the best-known authorities on dreams is Calvin S. Hall, Director of the Institute of Dream Research at Santa Cruz, California, and the author of a number of books on dream psychology. "A dream is a succession of images, predominantly visual in quality, which are experienced during sleep," Dr. Hall writes in *The Meaning of Dreams*. He views dreams very much like stage plays. "A dream commonly has one or more scenes, several characters in addition to the dreamer, and a sequence of action and interactions usually involving the dreamer. It resembles a motion picture or dramatic production in which the dreamer is both a participant and observer. Although a dream is an hallucination, since the events of a dream do not actually take place, the dreamer experiences it as though he were seeing something real."

This is a rather definite statement from what appears to be a specialist in dream research, and it is solidly based on Freudian concepts. Is a dream really not real at times? Dr. Hall dismisses or rather avoids any discussion of psychic dreams or astral projection, both of which contain elements of reality and are not hallucinations. Nor does the good doctor acknowledge the amazing cases of inspiration contained in dreams, in which seemingly unqualified or uninstructive individuals obtain specific information that leads them to invent things, to perform tasks for which they have not been schooled, and otherwise show evidence of external inspiration through the dream state. I am not referring here to the vaguely worded statements of poets and writers and musicians, that they are "inspired" by external sources, but to specific cases where entire projects have been completely designed through the channel of dreams.

"From our study of thousands of dreams, we know that they are relatively silent about certain kinds of conceptions and relatively vocal about others. Dreams contain few ideas of a political or economic nature. They have little or nothing to say about current events in the world of affairs. I was collecting dreams daily from students during the last days of the war with Japan when the first atomic bomb was exploded, yet this dramatic event did not register in a single dream," writes Dr. Hall.

To begin with, his statement as to the absence of political or economic ideas in dreams is patently false. As will be shown in some of the material presented in these pages, it is exactly such material that pervades the dreams of those capable of prophetic expression. As to the absence of registering a specific event even though the experimenter expects it to be registered, this is like saying, "Why doesn't the medium get my uncle Joe?" when I want her to get him. Surely we must judge results on scores, not try to explain why they don't score when we want them to.

Dr. Hall considers dreams primarily authentic records of a mind made anxious by conflict, that they are due to our inability to solve our problems in the waking state.

A somewhat different approach is taken by Erich Fromm, internationally recognized authority on psychology and author of a number of works, among which I consider *The Art of Loving* perhaps the most monumental contribution to human understanding. In a recent book entitled *The Forgotten Language,* Dr. Fromm says that it is more important to deal with the understanding of dreams than with their interpretation. He considers dreams to contain symbolic language, which he calls a language in its own right, "in fact the only universal language the human race ever developed," and he sees the problem of dealing with dream material one of understanding this symbolism rather than looking for some artifically created code. "I believe that each understanding is important for every person who wants to be in touch with himself, and not only for the psychotherapist who wants to cure mental disturbances." Dr. Fromm goes on to quote from the Talmud, the sacred Hebrew book of learning, "a dream which is not understood is like a letter which is not opened."

Where Dr. Hall flatly refuses to recognize dream material as anything but hallucinatory, Dr. Fromm says, "The dream is present, real experience, so much so, indeed, that it suggests two questions: what is reality? how do we know that what we dream is unreal and what we experience in our waking life is real?" The Italian playwright Luigi Pirandello has fashioned several dramas on this theme. Where Freud and his disciples tended to look to dreams as expressions of unresolved libido conflicts, Fromm sees in them symbolic material, which, incidentally, is identical no matter what background the dreamer may have, no matter what kind of people are concerned. A truly universal form of expression, Dr. Fromm feels that the symbolic language of dreams is "a language in which inner experiences, feelings and thoughts are expressed as if they were sensory experiences, events in the outer world. It is a language which has a different logic from the conventional one we speak in the daytime, a logic in which not time and space are the ruling categories, but intensity and association."

But dreams are all of those things, and more. To begin with, the dream state covers such a large segment of human experience that it nearly rivals the waking state, although it may occupy only a fraction of the conventional time spent by humans while awake. I consider the dream state a state of *heightened receptiveness*, necessary to convey to humans certain information which they would normally not accept because of the nature of their psyche. In order to perform effectively in the waking state, the unconscious part of the mind is generally shut off or largely subdued. Were it not so, humans would not be able to function as efficiently as they frequently do. On the other hand, concentrating one's energies on purely mechanistic actions results in the suppression and shutting out of the more gentle vibrations of a creative-perceptive nature. Thus it is necessary to have two sets of circumstances if humans are to function properly on *all* levels.

We already know what happens to the human body when we are asleep; the unconscious part of the mind is allowed free range of expression, while the physical body continues to function on a reduced scale, maintaining vital functions by an ingenious system, allowing just enough activity to maintain life, but not enough to intrude into the sleep state. At least, not in a fully balanced, healthy individual. The two other components of human personality, mind and spirit, or psyche, are, however, not necessarily dormant. Freed from the necessity of operating the body vehicle, they can turn their energies toward goals which they are incapable of pursuing when they must look after the body. As far as mind is concerned, as the "guardian of the vehicle," the natural task seems to be the filtering of information from outside, allowing it to come through and reach the unconscious level of mind in order to be understood by the dreamer. A degree of filtering is involved in order to make the material acceptable to the individual. On the other hand, the psyche, or spirit, is now free to send symbolic material upward toward the conscious level so it can be understood when the dreamer awakes.

We thus have a two-way traffic, external material being received and sorted out, and internal material being sent out to the dreamer's conscious, in order to call his or her attention to certain conditions of which he or she is not normally aware. Both processes use imagery in order to express themselves, supplemented by seemingly auditory material, that is to say, the dreamer not only sees scenes but also hears sounds, or feels that he or she does. Since no one else outside the dreamer either sees the same scenes or hears the same sound, they are evidently produced internally, stimulating the respective brain centers directly without the need to go through auditory or visual organs of the body. In a way, this is similar to transferring recordings from one machine to another without the use of an external microphone. The transfer is much the better since unwanted external noises are thus totally eliminated. The dream circuit is also direct and therefore more powerful than if the material were to go through external picture or sound sources.

I have divided the dream material into four major categories: dreams due to physical problems resulting in nightmares or distorted imagery, dreams due to suppressed material and useful for psychoanalytical processes, dreams of a psychic nature, and, finally, out-of-the-body experiences also referred to as astral projection.

As far as physically induced dreams are concerned, there is little quarrel among psychiatrists as to their reality and frequent occurrence.

When the body mechanism is loaded down with poisonous substances, through overeating, or other malfunctions of the system, these processes can indeed "press upon" the respective nerve center and cause nightmares or other forms of biochemically induced traumas, albeit of short duration, ending with the restoration of balance in the physical system or the awakening of the dreamer. Even ordinary states of discomfort, such as the need to void, can cause this kind of dream. Only Gypsy dream books would attach importance to expressions of this kind. But it is interesting to note that Dr. Hall sees a connection between such physical dreams and possible paranormal material. In discussing the ancient belief that dreams are produced "by the distemper of the inward parts," he speaks of dreams indicating future illnesses as *prodromic* dreams. The word comes from the Greek for "forerunner" and is interpreted by Dr. Hall as "a premonitory sign of disease." In this ancient belief, dreams of being suffocated or crushed, or of flying, were supposed to indicate the beginnings of a lung disease. Dr. Hall puts emphasis on environmental factors affecting the sleeper as being responsible for certain types of physical dreams, such as a room which is too cold or too warm, or which does not contain enough air, and so on.

It is important to realize that dreams caused by physical pressures do in no way relieve these pressures, nor do they in fact contribute anything to the sleeper's well-being except perhaps by notifying him or her of the existence of some disturbance in the body or environment. This is not surprising since I consider them due to a purely mechanical chain of reactions in the biochemical system of the body, not under the sleeper's control at all, or due to any kind of external forces. The physical system is out of balance due to one or the other cause, and the apparatus reacts in order to call attention to its plight. The moment the system is in balance again, the need for this action no longer exists and the physically induced dreams cease.

Dreams of the second category, due to suppressed material, are the grist for the mills of professional psychoanalysts. If the analyst follows the Freudian line of thinking, he or she will see suppressed libido and sexual symbols in every dream, and will explain the dreams on the basis of sexual maladjustments, needs and symbolisms. If the analyst is a Jungian he or she may do so in a number of cases which are sexual in content, but may explain other dreams as wish-fulfillment dreams or symbolic expressions along the lines of Dr. Erich Fromm. There is no gainsaying that dream material is a valuable tool for psychoanalytical interpretation, that psychoanalysis itself is very useful in many cases. But it is most useful when we are dealing with psychoneurotic individuals, because a psychoneurotic can at times be cured through discussions of his or her suppressed problem. Not so with the psychotic individual, who is much less accessible to discussions of this kind. In that case the dream material becomes merely an informative tool to the doctor, but the two-way dialogue is either non-existent or very much restricted and practical results are therefore harder to obtain.

It is not the purpose of the present book to go into the question of psychoanalytical dream interpretation, except to say that a certain percentage of all dreams do belong in the category of such material, while an equally large and impressive number of dreams do not. Unfortunately, very few trained psychoanalysts understand the difference between symbolic dream material and true psychic dreams. They deal with psychic material as if it were simply symbolic material and as a result distort the interpretation. This is of course due to the fact that the majority of clinical analysts and psychiatrists do not as yet recognize parapsychology as a sister science, or if they do, are not properly trained to apply its principles to their own work. Individual psychiatrists and analysts who do know parapsychological methods are far in between, and the need for more massive training of up-and-coming specialists in this field seems very great. I recall going through psychoanalysis myself in the late 1940s at a time when I was under great external pressure, and thought that analysis would help me understand myself better. My therapist was Dr. E., who had been an assistant to the great Carl Jung. We spent a great deal of time looking over my dream material, and the doctor's method consisted in my first interpreting my own dreams, after which he would interpret them as he saw the material. There were a number of psychic dreams in the lot, and invariably, we came to different conclusions as to their meanings and derivations. After six or seven months I discontinued the sessions, and did not meet Dr. E. until many years later, when Eileen Garrett sponsored a psychotherapy forum in New York City. "I am happy to see you here," Dr. E. said when he recognized me. I shook my head and replied, "No, Doctor, I am happy to see *you* here." Indeed, Dr. E. had become interested in the work of psychotherapy as practiced by leading parapsychologists of our day.

Before we turn our attention to the remaining two categories of dreams, that is, psychic dreams and out-of-the-body experiences, it is well to state what the differences are between these and conventional dreams. Dreams due to physical discomfort or environmental pressures and dreams of a psychoanalytical connotation are not nearly as vivid as psychic dreams or out-of-the-body experiences. The first two categories of dreams are more easily forgotten upon awakening unless they are immediately written down. Not so with psychic dreams or out-of-the-body experiences; one is rarely able to shake them, even if one does not write them down immediately. Some psychic dreams are so strong that they awaken the dreamer, and in most cases I am familiar with the dream remains clearly etched into the memory for long periods after the dream itself has occurred. Also, with dreams of categories one and two, so-called impossibilities occur with great frequency. Perhaps Dr. Hall's statement that dreams are hallucinatory and not real is understandable in the light of the nature of such dreams. Clearly, dreams in which impossible events take place, mostly out of ordinary time and space sequence, must be hallucinations; but psychic dreams and out-of-the-body experiences are nearly always completely logical sequences of events, frequently entirely possible in terms of ordinary logic, and are received by the dreamer with a sharpness and clarity the first two types of dreams are not.

Although all four categories share a common denominator, that is, the dream state, the first two categories are jumbled, sometimes very confusing bits and pieces of information, while the latter two categories are nearly always complete messages or events, devoid of the fantasy trips and sleight of hand so common with the first two categories of dreams. Of course, there are cases where the categories of dreams get intermingled, and purely symbolic material may become superimposed on true psychic material. This happens where a dreamer is not fully relaxed, or is not a very good recipient of external material. But a skilled parapsychologist can differentiate between the portion of the material properly belonging to category one or two and that representing authentic psychic material.

PSYCHIC DREAMS

A psychic dream is a dream in which material from an external source or from an internal source not ordinarily active in the conscious state is received. In the vernacular, this means that psychic dreams contain information from messages, warnings or other communications from individual entities outside the dreamer's consciousness, or they may contain material obtained through psychic abilities of the dreamer him/herself, abilities which he/she does not normally use in the waking state. This is the main body of the present work, really, a much neglected aspect of dreaming. Although the evidential material in this particular field is nearly overwhelming both in scope and amount, comparatively little of it has found its way into the supposedly authoritative works on dreams and dreaming presently used as textbooks.

Norman MacKenzie, in *Dreams and Dreaming*, published in 1965, devotes a few scant pages to paranormal dreams as such, unearthing the old chestnut about Abraham Lincoln's premonitory dream of his death, and Bishop Joseph Lanyi's dream of the assassination of Archduke Franz Ferdinand in 1914. MacKenzie writes, "The difficulty is that no aspect of dreams is more intriguing and less amenable to systematic inquiry. It may not be impossible to set up significant experiments to test the extent and character of such dreams, but it is very hard and such experiments are still in the earliest stages." Norman MacKenzie is not a doctor, but essentially a journalist, although he has taught sociology in England and the United States. For a knowledge-able writer to say in 1965 that "experiments are still in the earliest stages" shows a monumental lack of knowledge and understanding of parapsychology. By the middle sixties tremendous amounts of material had been gathered both at Duke University and other centers of learning, Professor Hornell Hart had already undertaken his famous dream experiments and published them, and material was freely available to those seeking it. As for Professor Hart's dream experiments, they consisted in a methodical survey of the dreaming habits of 300 students under his control. The participants were required to allow themselves to be awakened at regular intervals, and to record their dream experiences. From this Professor Hart later concluded that many of the dreams involving the apparitions of the so-called dead were in fact veridical, and that these apparitions were what they claimed to be, i.e., the spirits of the dead.

George Nobbe, in the New York *News* of November 2, 1969, undertook a popular survey of dream research then going on. At that time the so-called Central Premonitions Bureau in New York City, headed by R. B. Nelson, served as a channeling organization for premonitory dreams. My own organization, the New York Committee for the Investigation of Paranormal Occurrences, founded in 1962, also had accumulated a significant number of such dreams. Nelson breaks down his material into eleven categories, from death and disaster, news, prominent personalities, natural disasters, war, space, politics, and so forth, to a special category for the Kennedy family. This, of course, is not a scientific approach but simply a convenient arrangement. Nevertheless, some impressive cases are quoted, such as the dream of a California lady that the United States would be attacked by a foreign country somewhere in Southern California. Incredible and as unlikely as the dream was, a few days later a Mexican vessel fired on a tuna boat in the Pacific Ocean near San Diego. Another contributor to Nelson's office reported a dream concerning illness aboard spacecraft *Apollo 7* and difficulty while landing. It turned out later that the spacecraft came down upside-down in the Pacific, and that the crew was suffering from colds. Far from making light of investigation into paranormal dreams, the article quotes Maimonides Hospital experimenter Dr. Stanley Krippner and an article of his authorship in *Psychoanalytic Review*, "Paranormal dream data collected at the Maimonides Medical Center include several incidents of precognition."

Katharine Cover Sabin, in *ESP and Dream Analysis*, begins to bring some common sense to the vast field of psychic dream material. "The psychological dream factors discovered by Freud do not rule out precognition in dreams; instead the dream psychology often forwards the parapsychological content. Dreams can be realistically true or symbolically true. Gifted psychics are more prone to receive understandable predictive material than non-psychics who usually receive dream guidance through symbols. However, both the gifted and the ungifted should make a study of dream symbols, for parapsychological material is most often presented symbolically."

This is only partially correct. An impressive number of dreams are devoid of all symbolic material and present events in the dreamer's life or in someone else's life which have not yet transpired, but eventually do, precisely in the same manner and in detail as foreseen in the dream state. In fact, to accept symbolical dream material as indicative of precognition presents a somewhat dangerous attitude; when it becomes necessary to interpret symbolic material in order to arrive at some clear-cut meaning concerning future events, the conservative or orthodox psychiatrist may justifiably reply that his/her interpretation is just as valid, or more so. Fortunately, there is an overwhelming body of "clear dreams" totally free of symbolic embellishments, and capable of immediate understanding by experts and laypersons alike.

"The future is not irrevocably fated. When we know the trend of the future, we can often avoid pitfalls or be led to opportunities," Sabin continues. She holds that there are four keys to the parapsychological content of dreams, namely, fixed symbols, association, the play upon words, and arbitrary coding. This is certainly a vastly superior method to pure psychoanalysis, especially as Sabin is a professional psychic herself and accepts the existence of discarnate entities, i.e., spirit. But it still uses the methodology of psychiatry with material which seems often hard to categorize, because so many dreams are applicable only to the individual involved and to no other. Sabin has developed special cards, which she uses with the help of computers to give dream interpretations. As the title of her book implies, she is primarily concerned with ESP content in dreams, but the ESP type dream is merely one of several kinds of paranormal dream occurrences.

The evidential material obtained through the mediumship of the late Edgar Cayce of Virginia Beach, Virginia, is so impressive that his views concerning psychic dreams should also be taken into account when evaluating a proper approach to psychic dreams. In his book *Edgar Cayce on Dreams*, Dr. Harmon H. Bro states that "in Cayce's view it was not only business details that would present themselves in advance to the dreamer and that any condition ever becoming reality is first dreamed. He meant, of course, major developments that were the outgrowth of the directions and habits of a life or lifetimes." Cayce also taught others how to dream constructively, as it were, and to recall their dreams upon awakening. Dr. Bro, in another work, entitled *Dreams in the Life of Prayer*, says, "It was the contention of Cayce in his hypnotic state that every normal person could and should learn to recall his dreams so that he might study them for clues for better functioning in his daily life." Dr. Bro remarks that later studies of dreams in the laboratory uncovered a remarkable ability shown by some subjects to interpret their own dreams while under hypnosis. "Had Cayce done his work several decades later, he might well have been studied for his hypnotic interpretations of his own dreams, if not the dreams of others."

Unfortunately, Cayce passed on to higher realms in 1945, at a time when research hypnosis was not yet as widespread or as fully recognized as a tool as it is today. Cayce believed that dreams should be studied in series, not just as individual dreams. Since Cayce never claimed credit for his own pronouncements, this approach must be credited to the "source" working through the entranced Cayce. "Using sets of dreams in this way, one could proceed as does a cryptographer:

using gains of interpretation made in one dream to illuminate others similar to it," writes Dr. Bro. Of course, since Cayce or his source used a unique system of looking at life, the Cayce view concerning dreams must of necessity also be specific and in line with his general thinking.

Although Cayce held that the great majority of dreams could be interpreted and in fact best interpreted by the dreamer him/herself, once he/she knew how to do this, Cayce himself also contributed a great deal to the interpretation of dreams of others. "As the entranced Cayce interpreted dreams," Dr. Bro states, "he began with their *function*. They could be found to operate in one of two ways—or in a combination of these two ways. Some dreams are primarily concerned with advancing the dreamer's practical effectiveness in the concerns of his daily life; these problem-solving dreams were the province of the 'subconscious' which held the dreamer's habits, functions, style of life and immediate practical problems. Other dreams were clearly concerned with changing the dreamer, with improving his commitments, and enlarging his self-image, enhancing his understanding of life, or even relating him better to God. Such dreams were primarily the province of the 'super-conscious' though mediated through the subconscious for the actual dream production on the stream of consciousness. Still other dreams contained elements of both kinds of dreaming: problem-solving and transformative. Such mixed contents might appear in successive portions of one dream, or more often in layers of meaning of the same dream symbols (as Freud so well demonstrated). In any case, dreams were 'answers' to the life of the dreamer."

Be this as it may, I have found that psychic dreams, or paranormal dreams, if one prefers this term, tend to be of certain specific kinds. I have therefore subdivided the subject of psychic dreams into six categories which seem to cover practically all the dream material available to me in my research. These six subdivisions are: *prophetic dreams*, in which future events are foreseen or foretold; *warning dreams*, in which future events are depicted in such a way that one can alter the results; *ESP dreams*, containing telepathic material frequently of simultaneous events or retrocognitive material, such as psychometric dreams in which events from the past unknown to the dreamer are experienced; *out-of-the-body experiences*, or astral projection, in which the dreamer or rather his inner, astral body leaves the physical shell and travels to events or places external to the personality; *survival dreams*, indicating communications with the world beyond or with discarnate individuals; and finally *reincarnation dreams*, in which experiences from other lifetimes are relived or memories realized which are not known to the dreamer in his/her conscious state.

Dreams have always been considered important; from the dawn of humankind, attention was paid to what humans dreamt, but the evaluation differed from culture to culture. Unfortunately, there was no distinction made between purely symbolic dreams and true psychic dreams, and astral projection was lumped in with the other dream material as well. Consequently, a great deal of significance was attached to dreams containing symbolic material pertaining solely to the individual dreamer, and having no relation to the future. This went to extreme lengths; the Bible and other ancient documents are full of interpretations, in which differentiation has to be made between the dream image and its meaning in the world of ordinary reality.

On the one hand, there were such clear-cut psychic dreams as that of Calpurnia, the wife of Julius Caesar, who told her husband on the day of his murder that she had dreamt of his assassination that night, that she had seen his statue in the Senate bleeding from many wounds. Caesar, however, rejected his wife's warnings as hysteria and went to the Senate, where he was assassinated by the daggers of many politicians.

Even less inclined to accept the generally prevailing attitude toward dreams was the philosopher Cicero, who expressed his doubts that dreams had any meanings whatsoever, and ventured the opinion that the gods had better things to do than to warn people through such unreliable means as dreams.

Philosophers of antiquity were like the conventional scientists of today: Aristotle could not accept the possibility that supernatural beings were in contact with humans through dreams, or that the soul could detach itself from the body during sleep as in astral projection. If anything, he was a skeptic. On the other hand, there was hardly a ruler of importance in ancient Greece or the Roman Empire who did not consult with an interpreter of dreams. The Bible is full of such incidents, beginning with the amazing rise of Joseph in Egypt and going all the way to the angel who appeared to Joseph, the father of Jesus, in a dream advising him that it was now safe to return to Israel since Herod had died.

But the second-century philosopher Artemidorus stated that "dreams and visions are infused into men for their advantage and instruction," and it is on his work that most of the subsequent dream books are based. However, Artemidorus went to great pains to explain that the interpretation of a dream depended largely on the interpreter, and not so much on the dreamer. Contemporary psychiatry and analysis put the emphasis on the dreamer, not the practitioner. In her book *Dreams*, Sandra Shulman makes an interesting point here. "Artemidorus preceded Freudian thought by nearly two thousand years when he wrote that dreams of excrement and mud signify wealth and treasure, an interpretation also to be found in the Assyrian Book of Dreams."

Artemidorus considered dreams from two points of view: ordinary dreams caused by mental or physical conditions of the dreamer and his/her environment, and dreams pertaining to the future, that is, containing material and symbols which could be interpreted to foretell events yet to come.

The ancients put great stock in omens, portents of events in the future which were not by themselves clear-cut or definitive, but which could be interpreted as having significance for either the one observing the omen, or sometimes entire groups of people. Omens are more in the nature of disguised warnings of things to come, sort of a bonus for those who can read the signs and benefit from that ability. Of course, the interpreter's point of view plays a significant role in the interpretation of such omens, if not his/her suggestions, which may in some instances help make the omen become a reality. I, myself, find the majority of omens far-fetched and the links between them and actual events in the future extremely tenuous. On the other hand, there are numerous instances of clear-cut visions obtained in the dream state that give details of future events that should render the dreamer capable of doing something about the impact of such an event. Why then should it be necessary to disguise so many warnings in frequently obtuse terms, poetic language, hints and other indirect forms of communication? I therefore regard the majority of such symbolic material as not objective *per se* but derived largely from the mind of the beholder. Examples include dreams of flying, which once were interpreted as signifying happiness, wealth and fame, if the dreamer landed easily, but if he/she fell and hurt him/herself, the dream signified the opposite. In the Far East it was believed that it was important to know the cause of bad dreams because that way one could get rid of fear or worry. Frequently, opposites were seen in dream actions, i.e., if one dreamt of taking something, it really meant giving or if one dreamt of being hungry, it really meant that one was more than satisfied. All over the ancient world, people were encouraged to sleep inside the sacred precincts of temples, in the expectation that the healing gods would descend and heal them in their sleep. Much of the results were due to suggestion, of course, but there are instances where psychic healing took place during sleep very much as it does in modern healing practices.

As the ancient world gave way to Christianity, much of the advanced knowledge concerning human nature accumulated by pagan civilizations was either lost or destroyed by the emerging Christian church. Although the early Christians accepted dreams and sleeping in specially constructed churches as part of seeking divine guidance, gradually dreams became suspect because so many of them seemed to by psychic in nature and thus were linked with witchcraft and the occult in general. As the church became less and less tolerant of other religions, dream interpretation became dangerous for those practicing it publicly. It did not stop people from interpreting their own dreams or seeking the help of "wise men or women," but it put the onus of potential official persecution on any public discussion of such material.

From very ancient times, however, there was one type of dream which escaped public condemnation if a civilization was bent on such condemnation. That was the dreamer in the person of the priest, the sanctioned dreamer, who would then provide his or her own interpretation. A good example is Pythia, the Oracle of Delphi, who went into self-induced dreams (caused to some degree by inhaling sulfurous vapors emerging from the earth) and who then interpreted these dreams for individual seekers, usually for a good fee. Needless to say, many of these interpretations were ambiguous and thus assured the continuance of the Oracle. Even during the Middle Ages, dreams by Christian leaders, or discussions of earlier dreams by the church's saints, were possible because they were considered divinely inspired, whereas dreams by ordinary people were suspected of being the work of the devil or demons. The subjugation of divination to political necessity is by no means restricted to the medieval church; even as recently as the period before World War II, the Nazi hierarchy consulted astrologers and dream interpreters, who had to be very careful with their interpretations lest they incurred the anger of their clients. Religion has always made use of dream material but for its own ends. If someone dreamt of future events it was divine kindness giving him/her a chance to foresee the event before it happened. Such psychic dreams were always considered extraordinary forms of intercession on behalf of the dreamer by a kind deity, or, if the content of the dream seemed threatening to the establishment, by demons or the devil himself.

Only in recent times have religious interpreters of dreams conceded the possibility of paranormal material occurring in dreams, of dream material originating from discarnate sources rather than being the product of superhuman creatures properly belonging to the realms of religion. But this is largely a question of semantics; those whom the church calls angels, or whom some religions call Masters, are not necessarily super-normal beings but simply particularly gifted human beings who have progressed to higher realms in the course of time. After all, angel only means messenger, and Master stands for one who is an authority in his/her field. The saints of the Christian church and others are in reality only human beings who have reached higher states of consciousness, due to their sufferings or greater enlightenment and because of their exalted state after death, may be called upon as advisors in need. Only in the popular mind have these figures taken on the status of demigods, miraculous personalities nearly as powerful as the deity itself.

Of course, a dream containing divine intercession does not necessarily reflect a true event. A devoutly Christian person may well dream that Jesus himself is contacting him/her in order to help or support him/her. In such cases the dream material may well be formulated by the dreamer's own unconscious mind as projected into the dream state. There is a real need for a Savior to show up, but only in the dream state does he/she assume form and a kind of objective reality. He/she may well be the result of projected thought forms, or a misinterpretation of a similar image, whereby the dreamer superimposes his/her preconceived "need image" on the apparition of a different personality from that of Jesus. I find it difficult to accept many of the reported intercessions by Jesus Christ in the dream state, not because I doubt the *possibility* of Jesus doing so if this were his desire, but because of the personalities, backgrounds and temperaments of specific dreamers reporting such dreams. In the final analysis, of course, one cannot be 100 per cent sure. As the late Bishop James Pike said, one must accept "the most likely of several hypotheses" when judging extraordinary events.

PROPHETIC
DREAMS

By prophetic dreams I mean all those dreams in which some element, some information is received pertaining to the future, as we know it. In essence something that could not occur by orthodox standards, but which nevertheless does. Prophetic dreams may range all the way from giant prophecies involving entire peoples or the world, to minor concerns of individuals pertaining to their own future or that of friends and relatives. What all prophetic dreams have in common is the element of future events that have not yet transpired, that have not yet begun to shape up in any form whatever, and which therefore could not be foretold by the use of the ordinary five senses.

A frequently heard criticism of prophetic material alludes to the probability factor, or informed guessing on the part of the psychically gifted person. Such arguments are easily disposed of. To begin with, no serious researcher in parapsychology takes a dream at face value unless it contains specific and detailed material of a nature that makes it capable of being verified later on. For example, a psychic announcing that a certain well-known statesman will be deposed or that some great luminary of the screen will remarry or that an aged politician will pass away is of no evidential value, because all of these situations have a high degree of likelihood. If they come to pass it does not disprove the psychic's ability, but it leaves a great margin of doubt whether the psychic was in fact drawing upon his or her inner resources or simply using his or her external reasoning faculties coupled with shrewd phrasing to make these "astonishing" predictions.

In some of my earlier works I made a distinction between prophecy and predictions in that I described prophecy as pertaining to major issues, worldwide situations and prominent individuals, whereas predictions might apply to anyone. A better term for foretelling future events is precognition, implying foreknowledge, whereas predicting means foretelling. Oftentimes the prophecy is visual or perhaps only intuitive and actual words are not used. The common denominator of this material is the future element, something that has not yet come to pass. It is essentially of little significance whether the information comes to the dreamer through visual stimulation, through verbal expressions, through intuitive feelings or through some other form of communication. The essence of it is that the message be clear, precise and sufficiently detailed to warrant the term of prophecy. Prophetic dreams, then, are dreams in which some event or situation pertaining to someone's future is contained and remembered upon awakening. Prophetic material can be obtained in the waking state, too, of course. I have already mentioned that a great percentage of psychic material in general comes unsought to individuals in the dream state because it allows for a deeper and easier penetration of the conscious mind shield. Due to upbringing or our modern approach to phenomena of this kind, most people apply logical values to psychic material coming to them, and in the dream state logic is absent. From the point of view of external individuals wishing to convey messages to human beings, it is easier to get through to them while they are asleep and ready for dreams, than while they are busily engaged in their daily activities. In the dream state, they have a human's full attention, even though he or she must wake up and remember in the end.

It is interesting that some individuals go through psychically active periods while at other times they are unable to have any ESP experiences or else sleep many nights without recalling any unusual dreams. Undoubtedly, the ability to have psychic dreams is connected with the receptiveness of the individual, which in turn has a relationship to physical states, mental conditions and environment, if only concerning the "instrument" through which the material is received. Mrs. S. J. G. of Long Island, New York, explained, "I find that I go into psychic periods when almost every dream will be prophetic or I become more sensitive or even telepathic. I have also learned that if a dream of mine is prophetic, that the time limit in which it will come true is from within a few hours to around six years from the time of the dream."

Frequently psychic people like to have company: when a prophetic dream is particularly upsetting, they take some consolation from similar dreams by other psychics, especially by well-known ones. Mrs. G. dreamt that the United States would be attacked by an atomic power, and she was shown the areas in which the attack would occur. The dream occurred to her in 1970, and she took great comfort from a similar prediction published by me in 1968, according to which we would be attacked on December 29, 1970. Happily, this prediction turned out to be out of date, if not false. Equally unreliable is the date of a similar prediction made by celebrated Chicago psychic Irene Hughes, who foresaw such an event around 1973. But mediums frequently foresee events without getting exact dates, or they may be off by considerable spans of time. It would be foolish to dismiss some prophetic dreams just because the date for the predicted event has come and gone without the event transpiring. Mrs. G. says, "Although I have many prophetic dreams I can never be sure when one is a prophetic dream and when not. There is one clue: my prophetic dreams are very definite in their message. There is no symbolism, such as with most dreams. I see the events and actions as they will happen. The message is clear and not surrounded with symbols."

It is easy to see why "true dreamers," people gifted with the ability to foresee events in dreams, were considered in league with the devil in olden times. Mrs. G. had a rather unusual dream one night about a fire in the living room and the strange thing about that fire was that it ran up the wall. The following day she happened to be talking to her neighbor, Jean, and her neighbor's mother, and she mentioned the unusual dream she had had the previous evening. The mother gave Mrs. G. a terrified look and ran away. The neighbor explained that earlier that morning her little boy had started a fire in the living room which caught on the curtains and did indeed run up the wall. Fortunately, they were able to put it out in time. There was no way in which Mrs. G. could have had prior knowledge of this event.

Dr. Calvin Hall states, in discussing the meaning of dreams, "Dreams are purely and simply hallucinations." He goes on to explain that a hallucination is an event that isn't really taking place, and that "dreams are creative expressions of the human mind," again intimating that for some reason or other we manufacture our own dreams, that dreams are the product of humans. Dr. Hall, of course, has made no allowances for psychic dreams. He goes to great lengths to explain seemingly psychic dreams as expressions of human longings, needs, problems and so forth. But he doesn't explain how it is possible for dreamers to obtain exact knowledge of future events, details of which are not even in existence at the time of the dream.

One of the largest German newspapers is currently upsetting the apple cart of conventional beliefs with a series dealing with "second sight." Among the examples in this newspaper series is the story of actress Christine Mylius, who has dreamt true since age twelve. At that time she had a dream in which she saw her elder sister on the water but somehow in the Alps as well. Three weeks later her sister drowned in a mountain lake in Bavaria. Since that time Mrs. Mylius has registered a total of 2,439 dreams with Professor Hans Bender of the Freiburg Institute of Parapsychology. Her "dream journal," containing 200 pages of prophetic dreams, has just been published in Germany. These dreams contain correctly predicted traffic accidents involving her mother and her son, various suicides of friends and relatives and material pertaining to total strangers which nevertheless turned out to be true in the end. Mrs. Mylius also was very good with newspaper headlines long before the events took shape and of course long before the printer actually set type for the headlines of which she dreamt. On January 4, 1967, she correctly foretold and registered with Dr. Bender the headline pertaining to the *Apollo* catastrophe of January 27, 1967. The German dreamer notes that her most evidential dreams occurred to her when she was under emotional stress or pressure. With the realization of the dream material and her registration of it, the tension left her.

All kinds of people have "true dreams," that is to say, dreams that later come true. The ability spans every conceivable class of people, and there is absolutely no way of narrowing it down to any specific group of individuals. If anything, one might say that people who have no strong prejudices against ESP and who live fairly harmonious lives are more likely to have psychic dreams than others not so inclined. The difficulty with individuals undergoing psychiatric treatment or possessed of strong obstructionist views on the subject is that they would either tend to embellish dream material on reporting it or suppress it. A very fine example of a well-balanced individual who has shown an increasing amount of ESP is the artist Ingrid B., with whom I have worked on many occasions, investigating cases or experimenting with various forms of psychometry.

On March 8, 1972, Ingrid reported to me a dream she had had on February 29, 1972. "I had a dream concerning a man at work. I dreamt he came into my office, was wearing a plaid sports jacket and turtleneck sweater and said, 'How are you?' and 'We must get together for a drink sometime.' The next morning the same friend did come into my office wearing the exact clothes I had seen him wear and he said, 'How are you?' followed by, 'We haven't talked in a while so we have to get together sometime.' Except for the slight variation in the last line, the dream was completely exact." Since Ingrid's dream occurred only a day before the actual happening, one might conceivably assume that the thoughts of the event were already embedded in the unconscious mind of her friend. But there are difficulties with that explanation. While it might hold water for the clothes seen in the dream and actually worn by the man in real life, the choice of words could not have been pre-planned, even if the man had intended to visit with the artist.

Ingrid reported another dream, which occurred on January 29, 1973. In the dream she saw a girl friend she had not seen for almost a year. Ingrid was returning to her home on Staten Island from the city, and as she was walking along Battery Park, she saw her friend coming the other way. It was springtime, and the girl looked thinner and better than she had ever seen her look. Ingrid noticed that her friend was wearing an antique white dress with embroidery on the front. Behind her lagged a tall, thin young man with sandy hair. He was wearing dark slacks and a white shirt with rolled-up sleeves and an open collar. He looked rather bored. As Ingrid passed her friend, she called out to her but her friend stuck up her nose and said, "Who needs you anyway?" The dream seemed so unusual to Ingrid that she decided to call her girl friend to check on its contents. Her friend confirmed that she had been thinking of Ingrid the night before. Also that she had lately lost twelve pounds and had stopped seeing a steady boyfriend. The boyfriend she described as tall, with sandy hair and wearing the clothes Ingrid saw him wear in her dream. As to the white dress which to Ingrid looked like an antique nightgown, her friend confirmed that she owned such a gown but that it had been in storage with her mother. At the time Ingrid was having her dream, she was thinking of getting it back. From this it would appear that Ingrid, in the dream state, was able to tune in on her friend's thoughts and permit her own unconscious mind to report them to her conscious mind to be sorted out, and eventually take some sort of action, which she did by calling her friend.

A third dream reported by Ingrid seems also worth mentioning here. In September of 1974, Ingrid and her fiance had been thinking of buying an antique sofa, but could not find the right one. On September 10, 1974, Ingrid dreamt that she and her fiance went into the country and stopped the car in front of a house where they saw a woman wearing a simple housedress. The house had a door in the center, there was a very peaked roof and as the woman, in the dream, stepped onto the lawn, she said, "I have something for you." The dream was so vivid that Ingrid decided it had significance for the future. On a hunch, she decided to follow up on an ad she had previously seen in *Antiques Magazine*, telephoned the advertiser and discovered that this dealer did indeed have a sofa which looked like the one they were looking for. Under the circumstances, they decided to drive up that same weekend. "As we drove up to the house it appeared just as I had seen it in the dream. It was an eighteenth-century farmhouse with a door in the center of the eaves and the reason for the peaked roof was that it was actually a side entrance from the road. The woman was a simple lady wearing a flowered sort of housedress and I did buy the sofa."

Mrs. Susannah D. of New Jersey is a housewife who has had evidential dreams since age twenty. After her marriage she lived for a time at Lake Worth, Florida, but three months later the family decided to come back to New Jersey. The night before they were ready to leave, Mrs. D. had a dream. She saw a woman dressed all in black standing beside a car turned upside down, dabbing at her eyes with a white handkerchief. In the dream, the woman said to Mrs. D., "Please find my daughter, tell my daughter." Mrs. D. remembered clearly thinking in the dream that she forgot to ask the stranger for the name of that daughter, so how could she tell her? The following morning Mrs. D. told her husband of the dream and begged him not to leave that morning. She felt it was a sure sign from fate that they would have an accident. But her husband became irritated at the thought of delay and insisted that they leave as planned. They weren't out of the state of Florida yet when upon rounding a curve they noticed a long line of cars and police cars rushing by. They stopped, and looked to see what was the matter. Down in a gully was a car upside down, and a woman dressed all in black standing alongside, crying. Mrs. D. got out of her car and inquired what had happened. She was informed that the woman's daughter had been killed and was still trapped in the car.

Again, the dream content nearly fits the actual event, except that the information about the dead daughter was obtained from witnesses rather than from the woman in black herself. Nevertheless, this type of dream clearly shows that some individuals can tune in on future events before these events have become objective reality.

Specialist Fourth Class David P. had a dream which came true on *two* separate occasions. At age ten he dreamt that he was running on a lighted path, running from the lighted path into darkness. Now, such a dream can easily be explained as symbolic or of psychoanalytical significance. But young David went into the Boy Scouts and in his second year, in 1965, found himself at a summer camp. Coming back from a campfire one night, he had exactly the same experience as he had dreamt several years before, trying to catch up with the rest of his friends. The moon shone down as he ran on the path and the scene was exactly what he had seen in his dream. But then in February of 1972, when he was in the Army, he found himself in exactly the same situation again—the scene he had seen in his dream.

Mrs. Sandra M. is on active military duty with the Air Force, as is her husband. He works as an aircraft mechanic and she is a computer operator and both are twenty-five years of age.

Mrs. M. has had several veridical dreams. One that was particularly interesting occurred to her in July of 1970, when she and her husband were stationed at Travis Air Force Base in California. Their best friends at the base were named Darlene and Reuben, the latter stationed in Vietnam and at the time not due back for another six months. In this particular dream Mrs. M. had the impression that Reuben was coming home soon but that when he got to the base he could not find Darlene. He looked and looked for her but then left because he could not wait. Mrs. M. reported this dream to her husband upon awakening and later in the day also to her friend. It seemed an unlikely dream since Darlene hardly ever went anywhere, so the likelihood of her husband returning and not being able to find her was indeed remote. A month later Reuben came home on an emergency leave, unexpectedly, and when he got to Travis Air Force Base he could not find Darlene. So he left a note and went on to Santa Monica, where his grandmother was dying. Even though Darlene normally stayed around the house, that particular time she had gone square dancing and did not return home until after midnight.

Another interesting dream concerned a future assignment for Mr. and Mrs. M. In May 1971, she dreamt that she and her husband would be assigned to Robins Air Force Base in Georgia. At the time there were literally thousands of possible bases for them to be sent to, so it was not a question of informed guessing. In October of the same year, her husband's orders came through and they were indeed going to Robins Air Force Base in Georgia. At the time when she had had the dream, *even the Air Force did not know where to send them.*

These two dreams and others by Sergeant Sandra M. are attested to by her friends, and her service supervisor, so there is no doubt as to the authenticity of the reported material and the timing of it. A common criticism of dream material that later comes true is that people do not recall having dreamt certain things until *after* the event takes place: in this case and many others which I am about to report in this book, such a criticism would indeed be without foundation.

Frequently, events which come true at a later date cast a shadow ahead of them, and become known to individuals who have nothing whatsoever to do with the events themselves. Why this is so, and why certain individuals can thus tune in on future events which do not concern them personally, is hard to figure out. But there is an overwhelming body of evidence that it occurs, sometimes frightening the dreamer, sometimes merely puzzling him or her.

Mrs. Elaine F. of Chambersburg, Pennsylvania, had a dream in 1969, in which she saw a group of people having a party. They seemed like girl scouts to her and she herself was off in the trees looking on, while the group was celebrating. Suddenly some people came out of nowhere and began killing the "girl scouts." The killers were dressed in black and had bushy hair. In the dream she was particularly frightened by the eyes of the leader, whom she saw clearly. When she awoke the following morning, she described the scene and how she had seen blood running from the wounds of the victims. Ten days later the Sharon Tate murders broke into the headlines. As soon as Mrs. F. saw a picture of Charles Manson in the newspapers, she recognized him as the man she had seen in her dream earlier.

E. W. is in his late thirties, a chemistry graduate now working in another field. In January 1958 he was living in Florida with his parents, running a business with them. One night he had a dream in which he became aware of himself taking a shower, when the telephone rang. He waited a few moments to see whether his parents would pick up the phone, since they were usually up early, but since it continued to ring Mr. W. grabbed his robe and answered the telephone. In the dream he noticed that he ran to an upstairs extension in a room which was made up as if no one had slept in it for several days. He grabbed the receiver, which was on a small table next to the bed, and said hello. His mother's voice was on the other end saying, "Son, I am at the hospital with Daddy. He's dying. You'd better call the priest and get here as quickly as possible." And suddenly the strange dream ended and Mr. W. found himself wide awake in bed. He worried about the content of this dream, but decided not to mention it to his parents. At that time his father, seventy-three, was in perfect health and there was no reason why he should be in a hospital.

The dream occurred in January 1958. In late April Mr. W. noticed that his father seemed to have difficulty speaking. Eventually he took him to a doctor and it was thought that Mr. W., Sr., had had a stroke. But the diagnosis seemed uncertain, so Mr. W. took his father to a brain specialist in a larger city. There it was discovered that Mr. W., Sr. had cancer of the brain which was inoperable. They decided to drive back to Florida since there was nothing they could do about it. On the morning of July 15 of the same year, Mr. W. got up fairly early and jumped into the shower. He was just drying himself off when the phone began ringing insistently. He grabbed his bathrobe and answered the phone immediately whereas in the dream he had allowed it to ring for some time! His mother was on the other end of the line, saying the exact words he had heard her say in the dream many months before. "Son, I am at the hospital with Daddy. He's dying. You'd better call the priest and get here as quickly as possible."

Mrs. S. of South Bend, Indiana, had a strange feeling she should visit her grandfather, then living a hundred and twenty miles away in another town. One night she had a dream in which she saw herself in a house she had previously lived in. Her three sisters each had received a letter from a "Bert" but she hadn't gotten one. Next she saw people dressed in black standing around a grave. That was the entire dream, but the following morning her sister called and said that their grandfather had passed away the night before. His nickname had been "Bert."

Charles T. Glover, Jr., a native of Long Island, fifty-two years old, worked in advertising and publishing for ten years, and currently owns his own business as an antique restorer in Oregon. He has had a number of paranormal dreams through the years. Because of that he began to write down his dreams on the chance that some of them might later become reality. One such dream was as follows: he was riding on a train which, as it approached a city, went underground and finally came to stop beside a long, underground platform. He got off the train and walked along the platform with a large crowd of people. Ahead of him, in the distance, he could see a flight of stairs at the end of which shone the light of the outdoors. He went up the stairs and saw before him a roofed-over platform stretching into the distance with railroad tracks on both sides. On his right, in the dream, he could see a large city stretching to the horizon; but on his left he saw complete devastation—nothing but piles of shattered buildings and rubble. Then he awakened and recorded his dream. About a year later, in September of 1942, he went into the armed services and served in New Guinea, the Philippines and ultimately in Japan, where he arrived in September, 1945, and was stationed in a small town called Zushi, about thirty miles south of Tokyo. On his first weekend pass he decided to take the train to Tokyo. As he approached the city, the train dipped underground and finally came to a stop beside a long underground platform. As he joined the horde of people going toward a flight of stairs in the distance and finally began to climb the stairs, he had a strong feeling of *deja vu*. When he arrived at the roofed-over platform he recalled his dream in vivid detail. On his right stood the intact portion of Tokyo; and on his left were the results of many months of precision bombing by American bombers, aimed at the industrial sections of Tokyo—devastated right up to the railroad tracks.

Another dream seems worthy of being recorded here. In the summer of 1958 Mr. Glover dreamt he was sleeping in a tent beside a stream along with several other people in tents, sleeping bags and trailers. Behind the campsite was a tall, rocky cliff towering over the sleeping campers. Suddenly the earth began to shake and with a tremendous roar a great section of the cliff collapsed and came crashing down on them, burying them all in tons of rock and dirt. Mr. Glover related the dream in every detail to a friend also interested in paranormal dreams, Flora G. of San Francisco. Three days later the newspapers were full of an earth upheaval at Yosemite National Park. A campsite was buried by the very landslide he had vividly seen in his dream.

It is interesting to note that dreams, like other psychic impressions, sometimes reverse left and right or up and down, though not always. There is a very old tradition that one can enter the world of magic by stepping through a mirror, and that a mirror is in fact the borderline between the world of reality and imagination. It is of course a fact that our retina sees things upside down and straightens them up before forwarding the impression to the brain centers dealing with sight. In other words, we see the world upside down, but perceive it as right side up.

I am indebted to Mrs. Dixie B. of Winston-Salem, North Carolina, for the account of a friend, choreographer Peter Van Muyden. The two belonged to an experimental group that had been practicing meditation and various forms of consciousness expansion under the direction of Pastor George Colgin of the local Baptist church.

The dream which Mr. Van Muyden reported was the following: when he was a young man in Holland, he had the same dream several times. He saw a castle with a "freeway" in front of it and a river flowing beside. In the dream, he went through the gates, through a rose garden and into the castle. On the right he observed a stairway and in the middle of the stairs he saw an old woman. He went past her and saw two doors. He opened the door on the right and saw a room papered with Bordeaux red wallpaper, and a man hanging.

The dream made no sense to him at the time but many years later, by chance, he visited a castle and recognized it as the one of his dreams. There was the freeway in front, the river at the side, and the gates were the same, except that the position of the rose garden was reversed, as if seen through a mirror. When he entered the front door, the stairway was on the left. An old woman, the owner's aunt, did live there. He went up the stairs and since the garden stairway had been reversed from what he had seen in his dream, he decided to try the doorway on the left instead of on the right, and found it locked, but when he asked if he could see the room, he was told that the owner's aunt preferred to have it locked. It seems that the contractor who had renovated the castle had hanged himself in that room. When the room was finally opened to Mr. Van Muyden, he saw that it was indeed covered by the Bordeaux red wallpaper he had seen in his dream.

Now, the interesting thing about this dream is that the dreamer not only foresaw a future event before he had knowledge of it or before he had any contact with those who would eventually lead him to the place where the event would occur, but it even includes a tragedy, the contractor's suicide, which is subject to a number of imponderables. Nevertheless, the contractor hanged himself, and the dream became reality many years after the dreamer had perceived it.

Dreams of this kind seem to indicate an almost fatalistic sequence of events, even covering the seemingly free will and actions of other individuals totally unconnected with the dreamer!

Probably the least likely group of professionals to accept psychic material as true are magicians and other illusionists. There are a few notable exceptions where magicians have had experiences themselves which they cannot explain away. Such is the case of Barrie Schlenker, who works under the professional name of Vincent Barrett, and who makes his home in Lehighton, Pennsylvania. Billed as the man with the X-ray eyes, young Barrett presents a program of mentalist feats, which are frankly termed stunts and do not involve any kind of psychic ability. Nevertheless, on the morning of March 10, 1964, while he was living at home with his mother and grandmother, he had a dream early in the morning which he recorded upon awakening.

"The dream was one of those very vivid ones which seemed so very real at the time. I was dreaming that for a reason unknown to me I was driving my car in my bathrobe and pajamas. I didn't know where I was going, perhaps if I would have been allowed to finish the dream I would have found out, but I was suddenly awakened by the sound of a bell ringing with some strange note of urgency. I knew immediately what I was hearing: my grandmother had been ill for several years, she had had several strokes and many bad heart spells during that time, and I had built a bell pull system in our house so that if she needed help at any time she could pull a cord in any room of the house and a bell would ring in the stairwell loud enough for anyone else in the house to hear. This was the bell I heard on the morning of March 10,

1964. I got up as quickly as I could out of a sound sleep and went downstairs to see what was the matter. My mother and grandmother had gotten up about an hour earlier, had breakfast together and had been washing their breakfast dishes when my grandmother had suffered another heart spell. She sat down on a chair in the kitchen, never to get up again. Mother ran to the bell rope and rang it violently to wake me, which it did. As I ran downstairs I could see my grandmother propped up on the kitchen chair and I knew what had happened. My mother said I should quickly call the doctor and then go out in the country to get my aunt, mother's sister. I made the phone call and then without taking time to dress, just putting a coat over my shoulders on top of my bathrobe and pajamas, I got into my car and drove away, just then remembering my dream of only a few moments ago."

Dreams are by no means always harbingers of important events, nor do they necessarily contain messages of vital significance. In fact, the majority of dreams seem rather unimportant in the long view since they pertain to relatively unimportant matters. One wonders why the "powers that be" bother to allow people a glance into the future in such trifling matters. The answer, of course, is obvious: paranormal dreams are subject to laws just like everything else in nature. They are not the whim of individuals, even those on the Other Side of life. If an individual has the gift of psychic dreams, whatever material impresses itself on his/her unconscious mind at the time will be received and remembered upon awakening, whether it is important or not. There is no such thing as selective dreaming in this category of dream material, i.e., material pertaining to the so-called future, though there *is* direction in *some* forms of paranormal dreams.

Mrs. Judith White is in her early thirties and has lived in Massachusetts ever since childhood. She was married at age sixteen and lives with her husband and their three children. Her first paranormal dream occurred at age twelve. In the dream her right hand and fingers were swollen to about three times their normal size, and she remembers clearly not being able to move her fingers. This dream occurred to her six times. On June 11, 1955, when she was thirteen, she happened to be in an automobile accident, and among the injuries, the tendons in her right hand were cut. This required surgery and her hand was in a cast for a number of weeks, making it impossible for her to move her fingers. Unfortunately at the time she had the dreams she could not understand their significance, and thus was not really forewarned when the accident took place. In dreams where the significance of danger is realized, the percipient may be able to avert the incident or accident.

Sometimes paranormal dreams occur in spurts, and a person may have one and nothing at all for several years thereafter, when the ability resumes again. Whether this has to do with the need for paranormal dreams to be received, or whether this reflects changes in environment or physical and mental states of the dreamer, is hard to tell, perhaps a combination of both. After all, even the most renowned mediums have off days, when they do not function at all in terms of psychic receptiveness. When it comes to dreams with messages of some urgency, certainly the need to be received plays an important part in their frequency. In this chapter, however, I am dealing primarily with general psychic dreams, mainly the tuning in on future events without selective evaluation on the part of the dreamer and apparently spanning the entire width from very unimportant if not ludicrous detail to material of considerable significance to either the dreamer, someone known to the dreamer or someone not known to the dreamer who might be notified.

Thus it is by no means unique that Mrs. White should not have had any psychic dreams between 1955 and 1964, when the next event took place. In 1964 her mother-in-law was in the hospital, having been in rather poor health for a number of years previously, and in and out of the hospital. This time, however, Mrs. White had a vague feeling her mother-in-law would not come home. (Of course, such feelings could be explained on the basis of her conscious knowledge and her concern. Unless such feelings of impending doom are of a specific and detailed nature, containing data, dates, circumstances and such which could later be compared with actual happenings, it seems unreasonable to call them psychic, premonitory material, although they may very well be. We must keep in mind that alternate explanations are also possible and should attempt to explain events of this kind first by ordinary means, before turning to psychic avenues).One morning, while her mother-in-law was still in the hospital, Mrs. White was at the stage where sleep was about to end, yet she was not fully awake. At this moment she saw the entire family together, including her husband's brother who lived in California and whom she had never met. She had seen pictures of him, however. She had the feeling that they were all together because her mother-in-law had died. On March 22 her mother-in-law died and the family gathered together, including the brother from California. It was exactly as she had seen in her vision.

To illustrate how seemingly unimportant dreams of this nature can be, one of Mrs. White's more recent experiences serves as a good example. In her dream she saw herself sitting at a round table. With her were an unidentified woman and a man in uniform whom she did not know either. They were sitting there drinking coffee when Mrs. White asked the man his name. He pointed to a tag on his uniform which read "D. J. Brook." Mrs. White felt there was another letter at the end of the last name and thought that the name should be spelled Brooke. She asked him what the D. J.

stood for and he said that he was a disc jockey in the service. With that she awoke, wondering who the man was and why she remembered the dream so clearly.

Three days later Mrs. White happened to stop in at the local library to pick up a few books. After she returned home she opened one of the books she had selected at random and started to read. As she opened this particular book, the first sentence jumped to her eyes. It read, "The nameplate on the door read Dr. John Brooke."

Now, it is easy for the conscious or logical part of the mind to interpret, even in the dream, the initials D. J. as disc jockey. But why would so insignificant an event as reading a line in a library book selected at random for entertainment purposes be foreshadowed in a psychic dream? Again, the answer can only be that this category of psychic dream is an almost mechanical tuning in, at random, as it were, by the sleeper into the so-called future, not necessarily for any particular purpose. It may be compared to a searchlight mounted high on a tower scanning the beach below as a matter of routine; once in a while an object may be picked out by the searchlight and come to the knowledge of the person operating the light. More often, the light just scans the beach and nothing particular is observed.

Perhaps an even better example is a dream Mrs. White had on July 28, 1969. In the dream she saw herself drive up her street, when she observed some children running around near her house. Then she noticed the car next door in the driveway and the neighbors removing suitcases from the car, as they had returned from a month's vacation. On awakening she thought it strange that she should dream of the neighbors since they were not particularly close.

Three day later, Mrs. White and her family were returning home in her car when she saw the exact same scene happen before her eyes. There was no significance to it, nothing whatsoever. It was just that she had had a "routine" glimpse into the future. Fortunately Mrs. White feels rather sanguine about her ability. "I welcome any dreams or visions because I find the psychic world fascinating. I only wish other people would accept the fact that these things do happen. From what I have learned so far about this science it seems to me the main rejection is that people fear what they do not know. As for myself, I cannot know enough."

Many prophetic dreams foretell death or tragedy, but such subjects should not be confused with so-called warning dreams. In the case of warning dreams action may be taken to avert the outcome of the dream, whereas in the dreams discussed in this chapter, the events take place as foreseen, perhaps with minor changes in detail, but not in outcome.

An example of a warning dream which was not recognized as such, but which could not have been acted upon anyway, occurred to Mrs. Grace Middleton when she was vacationing in Denver, Colorado. In the dream she saw a casket in their local funeral home, and she noticed that the furniture, which had never been changed, was somewhat different from what she knew it to be. A davenport which had always faced the casket was now to the right side of it. As the dream continued, she saw her Sunday school teacher come in, and saw herself seated in the middle of the davenport. The teacher passed the vacant space to the left and in front of her and sat to her right. She put her arm around her and said, "I feel so sorry for you; I don't know what to do." Mrs. Middleton saw flowers with a large white lily cross in the middle. When the same dream occurred to her a second time, she told her husband about it, remarking that she feared something might have happened to her Sunday school teacher's grandson, who had been seriously ill when they had left town. She decided to write the Sunday school teacher a nice letter, telling her how much she meant to her and the church and town. When she arrived home, however, she found that her teacher's grandson was well, and under the circumstances, she dismissed the dream. Then, on September 26, 1952, her premonitory dream became stark reality: she found herself at the funeral parlor of her hometown, the furniture had been moved just as she had seen it in the dream and the flowers were exactly like the large white lily cross she had seen in her dream; but her husband was in the casket, having died suddenly from a heart attack, and her old Sunday school teacher was consoling her, uttering exactly the same words she had heard her speak in her dream two months prior to the event.

Here we have more than a premonition of an actual event that took place later, we have words selected by an individual which could not have been thought of before there was need for them to be spoken. The teacher could have chosen different words to express the same sentiment, yet she did not. What compelling force makes us use ideas and words in just such a way, and no other, and how is it possible that someone may have foreknowledge of our choice of specific words on specific occasions long before the occasions have arisen which would allow us to formulate our sentences in just that manner? Are we controlled by some powerful force of destiny, without realizing it, or do our independent, willful actions and thoughts cast a shadow ahead of what we call objective reality in such a manner that some individuals can become aware of them ahead of time? Such considerations seem to involve a re-evaluation of our concepts of time and space, possibly our positions in this continuum.

There is another consideration to be taken into account: to what extent are we *permitted* to obtain advance information on events which will later occur in our lives? I have no doubt that an orderly system exists, beyond the law of cause and effect as we know it, and that this system rules the nature and amount of information we may obtain concerning future events. From the material I have investigated over the years it seems to me that at times we are given exact advance information, while at other times we are given nothing whatsoever. In between lie the "veiled information" type dreams, not symbolic, but significant only in retrospect or to a very astute person, exhausting every conceivable avenue of interpretation.

In the case of Mrs. Middleton one should include a dream which she had shortly before her husband's passing. In that dream she saw her dead mother standing in the doorway of her bedroom, looking at her as if she felt very sorry for her. She had this dream three times in a row, and the day after the last occurrence of it her husband passed away. Obviously, her discarnate mother was aware of the impending death of Mrs. Middleton's husband, thus providing that the dead frequently have advance knowledge of events which we, in the physical state, do not possess except when we have psychic experiences. This does not mean that the dead are necessarily smarter than the living, but it does mean that there must be a reservoir of information upon which the dead can readily draw. It also proves that the system involving our departure from the physical world is a well-supervised setup, regulated by laws of which we know as yet very little. In other words, people do not die accidentally, nor does death occur unexpectedly, as far as "the system" is concerned. It only appears that way to us because we do not see the entire picture from our vantage point.

But the more we familiarize ourselves with psychic dream material and the possibility of it, the more likely we are to intrude into the area of foreknowledge and the more we will understand larger portions of the whole picture, both from the physical side and from the spiritual side of life. By being incarnate we are in effect cut off from knowledge of the entire picture, and only when we leave the physical body do we partake of the complete information concerning ourselves. Only the spirit entity is complete, while in the body it conforms to the limitations of a three-dimensional world which ordinarily excludes foreknowledge of events to come. During psychic dreams we are temporarily and partially able to pierce the "iron curtain" between the three-dimensional world and the full world of spirit, thereby obtaining bits and pieces of information which in the spiritual world are clearly visible to one and all.

Interestingly, paranormal dreams are comparatively frequent in young children. This is not surprising since ESP in general seems to be prevalent between ages four and eight, after which it frequently disappears, only to resurface around age seventeen or eighteen. A good case in point is Mrs. Sandra Staylor, of Chesapeake, Virginia. Now in her middle thirties, Mrs. Staylor is a housewife with two sons, and lives just outside Portsmouth, Virginia. Her husband works for an electric power company, and prior to her marriage, Mrs. Staylor worked as a cashier and bookkeeper. She clearly recalls her first paranormal dream when she was six years old.

Her father was building a house on a lot between their house and that of a neighbor, whose daughter was a year younger than Sandra. There was a pile of dirt from the digging of the foundation and it was near the property line close to the kitchen door of their house. The neighbor's girl and Sandra were playing on the dirt mound when the little girl said, "My aunt had a baby girl last night and she named her Nancy." The dream ended there.

A little more than a year *later* Mrs. Staylor's father purchased the lot between their home and that of the neighbor. Being a contractor by profession, he planned to build a house on the lot and then sell it. From the foundation digging there was a pile of dirt in exactly the place Sandra had dreamed. One day, the neighbor's daughter and Sandra were playing on the mound of dirt. While playing, the girl suddenly said, "My aunt had a baby girl last night." And before she could finish the sentence, Sandra said, "Yes, I know, and she named her Nancy!" This, of course, proved to be entirely correct.

It should be noted here that the intent to buy the empty lot had not yet come into the consciousness of Sandra's father, nor had the name Nancy been selected for the baby girl inasmuch as at the time of Sandra's dream the girl's aunt was not yet pregnant!

Sometimes paranormal dreams of this kind tune in on events in the distant future, sometimes into events only a few hours away. When Mrs. Staylor was in high school, she happened to be out of school for two weeks due to the flu, and was not in touch with the goings on at the school, including coming events. The night before she was to return to her class, she had a dream in which she saw herself giving an animal show in the school auditorium. She had snakes, an armadillo, a lion and many other animals to show. When she took the lion from his cage, a boy in the audience started roaring at him and the lion broke loose and went into the audience after the boy. All the children had to leave the auditorium and the lion was caught before he could hurt anyone.

The following day Sandra returned to school and that very same morning her home room and several others were taken to the auditorium for an animal show. A woman was giving it and she had all the animals Sandra had seen in her dream. When she took the lion from his cage, the boy sitting next to Sandra began roaring at him, the lion broke loose, and school authorities told the children to leave the auditorium. Fortunately, the lion was caught before anyone was hurt, precisely as Sandra had seen in her dream.

Here we have no element of warning, no particular gain from foreknowledge of the event, except in the nature of seeing a preview of a movie before the rest of the population has a chance to see it.

"I believe very strongly in God and feel that this is His way of warning us of things to come," Sandra Staylor explains, "I do not believe in predestination, I believe we create today what will happen in the future and God is warning us of the consequences of our actions. I believe that some predictions do not come true because the people involved see or are told what is coming and change their ways, thus changing their destiny." That, of course, is Mrs. Staylor's personal conviction, and based only upon her own experiences. Possibly, if she had access to other psychic dreams where the warning element was absent or where nothing could be done to avert a foreseen event, she might feel differently about the nature and reality of predestination or some sort of system setting things in motion which we cannot escape.

Regina Rudinger of New York City is a retired sales promotion executive. Late in 1932 or early 1933, she is not sure which, Mrs. Rudinger had a dream in which she dreamt that the entire department where she worked was being fired. At the time she was working as a clerk for a company associated with the New York Stock Exchange. In the dream the entire staff of the department was told one by one that they were being fired, which meant something like twenty people. The next day she told the other employees about it and was laughed at. But three months later the dream became grim reality. The entire department *was* eliminated and its work integrated with another department. The likelihood of this happening was extremely remote at the time of the dream.

Unquestionably, the so-called future is not a set condition, inflexible and inalterable. True, certain events are programmed for us to encounter, because our reaction to these events seems to be of great importance in determining our further progress. This is of particular importance in determination of karmic accomplishments or indebtedness. But there is some indication that the future keeps forming as we go along, and that perhaps a dreamer might be able to tune in only on part of it at a given moment, while at a later time he might see more of the so-called future. At any rate, I have on record an interesting dream reported by Sara McA., who at the time of the report made her home in Magnolia, Arkansas.

When she was ten years old, Sara had a recurrent dream in which she saw a certain house that she had never seen in her present life. There was nothing particularly outstanding about the house, but she noticed that a gravel road ran directly in front of it. Seven years later she happened to take a trip to a town she had never visited before. There, to her amazement, was the house she had seen in her dream, except for one detail: there was no gravel road in front of it as there had been in her dream. It so happened that the following year Sara took another trip to the same town, and again she found herself in front of the house of her dream. Imagine her surprise, when she noticed that the gravel road of her dream had now been completed.

It almost seems as if events are moving at a set speed along a time track and we, the actors in this unfolding drama or comedy, as the case may be, are moving on another band. At times we seem to be able to jump from our slower-moving track to the faster-moving time track and glimpse part of what lies ahead in our future, but which is in fact in the present as seen from the point of view of the faster-moving time track itself. The relationship between the psychic dreamer and events in the future is strictly relative and if we were capable of viewing both our progress and that of the events depicted in our dreams from an outside vantage point, perhaps we would be able to understand better the nature of what we now call, for want of a better term, the future. Unless we gain new understanding of the nature of time we will never be able to reconcile certain prophetic dreams with our natural, inborn view of a well-ordered, logically impelled universe.

Take as a good example a dream reported to me by my psychic friend, artist Ingrid B.

"The week of January 6-10, 1975, I had a vivid dream in which I went to an antique show and some dealer friends I knew were there. I had not seen these people for at least nine months and before I moved away from my previous apartment, we had not been on good terms. In the dream this man had some nice folk art birds which I had been wanting for a long time. I saw myself purchase one and hear him say, 'This is very good, you know, we've had it in our own collection for a long time.' That was the end of my dream. The following week, January 14, we did go to the show and the people I had seen in my dream were there and the folk art birds were there also just as I had seen them in my dream. As I was about to leave, the man said, 'I think you will enjoy these. You know they have been in our own collection for a long time.' "

Now, it would be preposterous to suggest that the exact wording of the antique dealer's parting message could have been made up in his mind a week earlier, before he even knew that a woman whom he had not seen in nine months would drop by his booth at an antique fair. Obviously, Ingrid was not reading the man's mind through some form of psychic divination, since the man's mind did not contain these thoughts or even any thoughts pertaining to her purchase of the folk art. On the other hand it seems equally preposterous to suppose that some super power in the beyond had directed her to go to the antique fair and at the same time ordained the dealer to speak the exact words which Ingrid heard in her dream a week earlier. There doesn't seem to be any particular significance to the entire incident, as it is, so we cannot see in it any deeper moral or other meaning, except perhaps to convince Ingrid that she could indeed foresee future events in her psychic dreams.

What then is the method by which many individuals can do this? Why are they able to do so? It appears from dream material of this kind that there must be some form of *impersonal* system in operation that does not distinguish between important and trifling dream material, which is put into operation almost mechanically if certain conditions prevail. What these conditions are we do not know fully as yet, but as we examine more and more verified dream material we may stumble upon a relatively simple setup explaining these extraordinary occurrences.

But it does imply a system in which a "pattern of destiny" is at work: nothing in the universe happens by accident or without good cause; surely, there is strong supportive evidence that the events in our lives are predestined to test our reactions to them, and if some of these events seem unimportant to us, it may just be that they are in fact of a different order of importance than the one we are used to in our evaluations of them.

Take for instance the case of Joan Adams of New York City. She is in her early thirties, the mother of three children, and her background includes some art, sculpture and music, though at present she is a housewife. Just before she turned nineteen she had a most peculiar precognitive dream. In the first half of December 1962, she dreamt she was sitting at a table opposite an unknown young man whose hair was very black. The surroundings seemed vague except for a white blurred background behind the boy. Suddenly, an arm with a fist shot out in front of him, startling him. As he gasped at the unexpected movement, Mrs. Adams then heard a girl's voice say, "It's an owl." At this moment she awoke, remembering quite vividly what she had dreamt a moment before. It made absolutely no sense to her, and under the circumstances she went back to sleep.

Two weeks later a girl friend, Barbara R., invited her to go to a New Year's Eve party in Brooklyn. Mrs. Adams did not know anyone else who was going and she had never been to the house. At one point during the evening several of them were sitting around a table, talking. Barbara was next to Mrs. Adams and a boy sat opposite her, while his girl friend stood behind him in a very old style fluffy white dress with ruffles. Then the exact sequence occurred as it had in her dream, without the slightest difference. The arm shot out and the girl said, "It's an owl." But whereas the dream had ended there, in real life there was something more: in the girl's fist there was a tiny wooden owl, which she was showing.

Again one could question the purpose of this precognitive dream, except perhaps that the expectancy, unconscious though it might have been, concerning Mrs. Adams' New Years Eve plans might have produced the dream to reassure her that she would not be alone, or that something pleasurable was in store for her. But that would presuppose some external agency causing Mrs. Adams to have this particular preview of events to come. The moment a significant purpose lies behind the psychic dream, we must include the probability of an external agency, if not a person then at least some form of law, causing the dream to happen for a purpose.

The overwhelming majority of dreams I have placed in this category of psychic dreams does not require any extensive interpretation on the part of the dreamer. They are more like the relaying of a message from the unconscious state to the conscious state, in the expectation that it will eventually materialize precisely as it has been dreamt, or as close to it as possible.

But there are occasional dreams which call for some sort of judgment, even symbolic interpretation on the part of the dreamer. Mrs. Helen J. lives in New York State with her husband. On March 12, 1964, immediately upon falling asleep, she had a dream in which she saw herself awake to the ringing of the front doorbell. She hurried downstairs wondering who it could be, as she knew her husband and three sons were at home at the time, sound asleep. When she drew back the curtain on the door to see who was outside, she froze with terror. "Although I couldn't see anyone, in one split moment I became aware of the 'Spirit of Death' on my porch. I knew I could never keep him out and at the same moment I could actually feel a great sense of compassion flowing from the Spirit of Death into me. In panic I fled upstairs to my bedroom and felt compelled to open the window." As she did so, still in her dream, she saw the scene of an accident, with a crowd of people, police and ambulance. She began to scream and woke up in her bed, still crying. She turned on the bed lamp and looked at the clock; it was exactly 11:30 P.M.

She then fell back into a troubled sleep. The following morning she told her husband that they would hear of a death, and all day long she felt uneasy and apprehensive. That night, Friday the thirteenth, her son David, aged sixteen, was killed in a highway accident at approximately 11:30 P.M.

After her son's death, Mrs. J. had his portrait painted from school pictures and hung it on the wall in her bedroom. On December 27, 1967, she had a dream in which she saw herself enter her bedroom and walk over to look at her son's portrait. His hair had been a beautiful golden blond, and so it was in the portrait, but as she stood there looking up at it, the color of the hair in the painting gradually changed to a light brown shade. At this instant she "knew" that one of his friends with light brown hair would soon be dead. Again, she told this dream to her husband and a friend of hers, Mrs. B. K. Four days later, on December 31, 1967, Specialist Fourth Class G.W. was killed in Vietnam. He had been her late son's closest friend and his hair was the same light brown shade Mrs. J. had seen in her dream.

The painting of her late son became a focal point of further dreams. In April 1968 Mrs. J. dreamt she was standing before it. She seemed to be speaking to someone, saying, "This is my son David." Suddenly his face became alive in the portrait and he bowed his head with eyes closed. The next instant real tears flowed out of the portrait and formed a large pool at her feet. She felt herself fainting and fell to the floor unconscious. Upon opening her eyes, she saw her family doctor bending over her, holding a hypodermic needle. At this point she awoke. Again, she related the dream to her husband and two friends. A week later she awoke with a lump on her leg and had to be admitted to a nearby hospital, because of a large blood clot. She spent nine days in the hospital, taking many hypodermic injections as part of the treatment.

At times, a psychic dream may not concern the dreamer at all, but pertain to other people. Sometimes the principals of the dream are not even known to the dreamer, occasionally there is a connection. A case in point occurred to Charles S., supervisor for the telephone company, who makes his home in Florida. On the morning of February 13, 1974, he had a three-part dream. In it, he saw himself standing in the street looking for his car. A person whose face he could not see told him that people thought he had been killed in an accident and that his car had been taken away to the funeral home. In part two of the dream he saw himself standing in front of the funeral home, looking at his car. It was the 1959 Dodge which he then actually owned, except that in the dream the car was white, when it was actually blue. Now, the 1959 Dodge has rather high rear fenders. There were some people standing around in the dream, saying it resembled the tail section of an airplane. In part three of the same dream, Mr. S. was standing in the funeral home, talking to a man and explaining that he had not been killed in an accident. At that point he could see four coffins: in one he could see a man and in another a woman. They were neither very young nor old. However, be could not see their faces clearly.

At this moment the alarm went off and Mr. S. awoke. At work, he thought about the dream, trying to figure out what it meant, but he was unable to come to any conclusions. He also discussed it with his wife that evening. The following morning, February 14, 1974, he learned that on the previous afternoon four people had taken off in a white airplane from a nearby airport. Two minutes after takeoff the plane had plunged to the ground, killing all four instantly. Although Mr. S. did not know the four people intimately, one of the women killed was the daughter of a very good friend who also worked for the telephone company. He had met the young woman and her husband once before, but had never met the older couple, their in-laws. In the dream he could not make out the faces of the older couple. Evidently this message, if that it was, had somehow come to him in the dream state because of his relationship with two of the people involved, although there doesn't seem to be any clear-cut purpose to it.

Not all recurrent dreams connect with reincarnation material, although the majority do. Mrs. Hazel W. is a housewife living in Alabama. She is twenty-nine years old, has three preschool children, and her husband works as a computer programmer. Mrs. W. had a dream which came to her several times: first when she was living in Alaska in 1969 and again in 1970, in Washington, D.C. In the dream she saw a bridge made of wood with planks falling off it. It seemed to cross a small stream with gurgling water, going over rocks. In the dream she saw herself standing on the bridge wearing a red and white dress, and there was a bright moon. There was a man nearby but she could not see him. In the dream she started running across the bridge, when he called, "Be careful!" She removed her shoes and ran back toward him. With that Mrs. W. awoke.

The dream made no sense to her, until she and her family moved to Alabama in 1973. On April 11 of that year, she was driving near Tuskegee with a friend, when they came to the very same bridge of her dreams. The incident occurred exactly the way she had seen it, proving it to be of a precognitive nature. Nothing spectacular followed, but it is interesting to note that in real life when she met the man who was driving her, she wasn't able to recognize him as the same man she had previously seen in her dreams.

Some precognitive dreams are real beyond being merely pictures or informative material pertaining to future events, and include physical sensations concerning these events as well. Mrs. B. R. is a housewife in her middle forties living in New Jersey. She has been enrolled in college twice; when she was of college age, and then recently in order to obtain a bachelor's degree.

One Sunday night in April 1942, she had a very realistic dream. The dream was about a classmate, R. L. Mrs. R. had not been talking to him prior to the dream or even thinking about him, since he was not a close friend. However, in the dream she saw him shot by a soldier and even felt the bullets in her own back, so strongly that it woke her up. She had never had a similar experience before.

In the morning, she told her parents about the dream, and found a sympathetic ear since her mother had also had precognitive dreams. In addition, she told several friends in school about the dream. Although the dream disturbed her, she assumed that it had been caused by the wartime stories prevalent at the time and could not possibly mean anything in relation to R. L., since he was only sixteen years old and too young to be in the Army. All week in school she looked at him with a new sense of awareness, but she did not mention the dream to him because she thought it would be in bad taste.

That Friday evening, R. L. and a friend, E. H., were going to Hackensack, New Jersey with E. H.'s parents. E. H.'s father was driving the car, and he took a shortcut along a street behind the Teaneck armory. He evidently did not realize that the armory, because of wartime conditions, was then under Army security and use of the street behind it was prohibited. When a sentry called halt, E. H.'s father apparently did not hear, since he did not stop. The sentry fired several shots at the car. The bullets hit the license plate and ricocheted off, hitting R. L. in the back, though no one else was hit. R. L. died the next day at the local hospital.

Some dreams seem to indicate that their purpose might be to contradict the expected, that is, they occur to a psychic person in order to "bring through" information that runs contrary to what the recipient might expect to happen. Mrs. B. R. also had a dream in August 1943 in which she saw a neighbor, B. W., get off a bus at the corner in their hometown in New Jersey. He wore a naval officer's uniform with gold buttons. Now, she knew at the time that he was stationed in Iceland, ferrying planes, and so when she mentioned to the young man's mother that she thought he would be coming home soon, the mother shook her head and informed her that her son was not eligible for leave for at least another year or more. Two days later, nevertheless, B. W. arrived in his hometown due to an unexpected trip to a Long Island airfield for emergency repairs. It gave him just enough time to hop a bus to New Jersey and visit his mother and neighbors.

C. Lane, who describes himself as "retired military," age fifty-eight, and who lives in New Hampshire, has had a number of unusual dreams. As any man with a military background would, he has kept an exact record of them, and while some of them have not yet come true, others have.

Sometime in the spring of 1969 he had the same dream twice in a row. He was standing by an airplane hangar and a plane on the runway wheeled and came toward him. Now, it was a fact that Mr. Lane frequently visited the so-called "fighter town hangar" near San Diego, when driving a navy vehicle to Miramar Naval Air Station. Eight months later, an airplane landed at that base, went out of control, and crashed into the very hangar where Mr. Lane had been standing in his dream. Several lives were lost.

On August 21, 1969, Mr. Lane, then living in Buffalo, New York, dreamt he saw a man attempting to bully and harass him. Three days later he went to work at a local company where he met for the first time the same individual he had seen in his dream. The man did indeed quarrel with him and bully him for several months.

On December 25, 1969, Mr. Lane had a vivid dream which he reported to me under the postmark of August 24, 1970. These dates are significant, since the events which the dream foreshadows came into being only three to four years later. In this dream Mr. Lane saw himself standing on the edge of an athletic field, talking with people around him. From out in the field to his right, he saw President Nixon coming toward him. As he passed in front of the dreamer and walked away to his left, the President suddenly became very thin and gaunt, looking emaciated, pasty-faced with red blotches on his face, and stumbled as he walked off the field. Since Mr. Lane, in 1970, was an admirer of President Nixon, the dream disturbed him a great deal. He wrote to a number of professional psychics all over the country, trying to fathom what the dream meant, but no one could tell him. Unfortunately, years later, it is clear what the prophetic dream about a stumbling President Nixon, walking away from the field of action really meant.

It is feasible that major political events, such as President Nixon's downfall, could cast rather strong vibrations ahead of coming into objective reality, for psychic dreams relating to these later events have occurred to many throughout the world. Mrs. May Siracusano, a housewife and mother living in Nebraska, reported a vivid dream under the postmark of May 26, 1970. In the dream she saw President Nixon at the White House, as she was visiting there with her family for some reason. Nixon appeared to her as a vampire, but since only she knew that fact, he was going to kill her in order to prevent her from telling anyone. She then saw a large stage on which a show was taking place, and there were many wax figures watching. Nixon in the dream, chasing Mrs. Siracusano, went among the wax figures, which fell down. Then the floor opened up and the figures disappeared into the opening in the floor, so that Nixon could not get to them. Meanwhile, in the dream, Mrs. Siracusano had gone to the FBI, for by now Nixon was raving mad, and the FBI took him away. That was the end of her dream, and in May of 1970 it made little sense indeed.

Anyone who doubts that precognitive dreams can disclose information concerning events and individuals whose existence is not a reality until well after the dream has taken place should ponder the type of dreams Mary S. of Houston, Texas has been having from time to time. Mrs. S. is thirty-two years old, a housewife with three children, who at one time worked in a bank.

Her first precognitive dream occurred in April 1969. At the time she did not know that she was pregnant. In the dream she saw herself holding a rather chubby baby girl with blond hair and blue eyes and she heard herself call it by the name Virginia. It was some time later that her family physician confirmed that she was pregnant, and so as a matter of course she prepared for a girl even though her husband insisted that it would be a boy. On December 30, 1961, her daughter was born. Her description matched the appearance of the baby in her dream 100 per cent and they did name her Virginia.

Apparently, dreaming of babies ahead of their arrival in this world turned into something of a specialty for Mrs. S. In June 1962, again before she could have known that she was pregnant, she saw herself and a baby, but nothing about it was clear and she wasn't touching the baby at all. She could not see its face, just a bundle that represented a baby. On August 7, 1962, she was taken to the hospital with a miscarriage.

In June 1962, she had the identical dream and sure enough, in late November she had a miscarriage again. Then in July 1965 the same dream occurred for a third time, except that this time she saw two bundles representing babies. Two days after Labor Day she lost twins. By now her husband became a firm believer in her dream ability. So when she had another dream in January 1966, he was ready to believe her. In this dream she saw a slender boy with dark hair, blue eyes, and a somewhat bluish color on his right side. She knew that his name would be Paul Ray. On July 20, 1966, a boy of that description was born to them; the bluish color on his right side was due to a Caesarean section. The name chosen for the boy was indeed Paul Ray. In January 1970 another dream occurred to Mrs. S. in which she saw two babies, both identical in looks: chubby with blond, curly hair, and blue eyes. One was a boy and one a girl, but she could touch only one child, not both. All during that pregnancy, the doctor heard two heartbeats. In August 1970 X-rays were made and disclosed only one child now even though the two heartbeats continued to be heard. On September 16, 1970, Mrs. S. gave birth to a boy matching the description of the boy in her dream, but there was no evidence of a second baby. She then recalled how she could touch only one of the two children in her dream, but not the other.

It seems the paranormal ability to dream true was inherited by this particular boy. At age four and a half he began to relate *his* psychic dreams to his parents. In August 1970 he woke up around one in the morning, screaming. After he had been calmed down by his parents, he spoke of a bad dream. He said he had seen everyone in the family in his grandmother's house, and they were crying. It was so vivid to him that he thought his grandmother had died. Before he would calm down entirely, Mr. and Mrs. S. had to telephone the boy's grandmother to satisfy him that she was all right. About a week later a telephone call summoned them to the house of the boy's grandparents; the boy's grandfather had suddenly passed away and the family was indeed assembled, crying. An identical dream occurred to the little boy in the later part of October 1970. Again the ominous telephone call informed the family that the boy's grandmother had passed away.

There is a category of psychic dreams which, on the surface of it, may more properly fit in with my category of warning dreams, because they contain an element of forewarning, usually of disaster or tragedy, which might be averted. That is, if the proper person to whom the warning applied could be identified. Unfortunately, in this category of psychic dream, the identity is not clearly given, so the connection cannot be made by the dreamer. As a result, the dream comes true as foreseen, leaving the dreamer feeling rather helpless and convinced that fate has been cruel in giving him/her this advance knowledge without the ability to do something about it.

Some of these dreams seem to be prophetic concerning events taking place in more or less the immediate neighborhood of the dreamer's house.

That is, there are a number of such dreams which depict events in the future, with which the dreamer has no connection, but which, nevertheless, occur within an area with which the dreamer is normally familiar.

A good case in point is a dream that occurred to Mrs. Margaret R. of Boston, Massachusetts, who is about fifty years old, a housewife and mother. Mrs. R. had a dream in which she saw a little yellow-haired girl, about three years old and wearing a white dress with small pink flowers on it. In her dream the little girl was standing at the curb, waiting to cross the street. As she started across, a black car came speeding toward her, hitting her with such force that her tiny body was tossed into the air and landed many feet away in a small huddled mass. She lay there without moving and Mrs. R. knew that the little girl was dead. No one moved to touch her. Finally, after what seemed an eternity, a cobbler came out of his shop, lifted the lifeless body gently, and carried her onto the sidewalk. The dream ended there. The dream was so vivid, Mrs. R. told her mother about it the next morning. All day long, she thought about it at work. When she arrived back home that evening, her younger brothers and sisters ran to tell her of an accident which had occurred just a short time before her return home. It was exactly like her dream, even to the pink and white dress, and it occurred in exactly the same spot she had seen in her dream.

Possibly dreams of impending disasters are more powerful, if not more frequent, just shortly before the event takes place. There are, of course, thousands of veridical dreams which come true months or even years later, but there is a sizable number of such dreams which occur within twenty-four hours prior to the event.

It seems to me that strong emotional events do cast a sort of shadow ahead of themselves, in some as yet not fully understood manner. Could it be that those who are responsible for such unfortunate happenings, are setting them into motion prior to their occurring in our consciousness? And are the dreamers perhaps tuning in on the thoughts of those originating these disasters in the next dimension, rather than on the disasters in the near future themselves? This, of course, presupposes that there is an orderly "board of directors" in the next dimension, planning our destruction or those of certain people, anyway, whose "numbers" are up.

Whatever the explanation, a case in point is a dream Mrs. R. had in 1944. She found herself standing in New York City looking at the Empire State Building. As she watched it, out of the fog came a passenger plane heading directly for it. She watched, horrified, as it crashed into the upper floors, flames spewing in all directions and pieces of the plane falling to the streets below. She could see the broken glass and parts of the building falling too. The next day, she read about this very event in the afternoon newspapers. Since she had told her family about her dream prior to it occurring, there is no doubt that her dream was of the precognitive variety.

There are psychic dreams which encompass more than one dream message, more than one incident. At times, one part of the dream comes true, and is duly registered as such, while the other part lies in the future.

An interesting case of this kind happened to Mrs. Marguerite P. of St. Petersburg, Florida. On December 12, 1971, she reported the following dream to me. She saw herself entering the White House in Washington, although she never had the slightest interest in politics or visiting the White House. She found herself in a large room in which she noticed a portrait of John Kennedy on the wall. There was a very long table in the room with chairs all around it. She sat down in one of the chairs and immediately all the other chairs were occupied. There was a man at the head of the table, with gray hair and a distinguished appearance, who was very angry. Mrs. P. heard him say: "There will be changes in the balance of power in Congress, due to elections and deaths of leaders. We must try to whitewash the scandal about the President, but I fear it will mean his leaving office." These words were followed by absolute silence. Then the men all disappeared and Mrs. P. found herself again alone in the room. As she left the White House, a young man passed, bearing a placard reading, "Mississippi New Negro State." Mrs. P. was justly mystified by the dream when it occurred to her, but since that time, the first part of her dream has become reality.

It seems that momentous historical events may "get through" to individual dreamers even if they have no interest in politics or in the public figure involved. This, of course, supports my view that this type of precognitive dream is not selective or individually directed but merely represents a random tuning in to the so-called future dimension. Since childhood, Mrs. Carolyn C. of Indiana has had a number of ESP experiences. But the experience she remembers stronger than any other occurred to her at the time when the late Senator Robert Kennedy was to visit her hometown in Indiana. It was during his political campaign, and he was to speak at a meeting to be held in a restaurant. Four nights prior to Kennedy's visit, she was awakened by a vivid dream in which she saw the Senator walk through a kitchen and someone shooting at him. The following morning she communicated her dream to her parents.

When Kennedy arrived in Indiana, he did indeed enter the restaurant, through the kitchen, and Mrs. C. thought, with some relief, that this was the subject of her dream. However, on the night of the California primary, she was getting ready to turn off her television set, when she suddenly felt she should watch the report from California. To her horror, she saw the shooting exactly as she had seen it in her dream. This scene, as we all know now, took place near the kitchen of the Hotel Ambassador in Los Angeles.

With the overwhelming amount of veridical dreams, psychic dreams which do come true, it is inevitable that there is a fair percentage that do not. This does not mean that the dreamer is making up the dreams, or distorting them in any way, but an ordinary dream based on impressions left in the unconscious may be mistaken for a psychic dream, or, if we are dealing with a genuine psychic dream, a date may be incorrect and the dream may yet come true in the future. However, to be considered evidential such a dream must contain a fair amount of specific, detailed information, not merely generalized statements. Betty B. describes herself as a professional medium, living in Brooklyn, New York. She has a good reputation and a fair-sized clientele. On October 16, 1972, she communicated to me a statement that she had seen, in three identical dreams, three days in a row, a newspaper headline reading, "Frank Sinatra Dead." Another strange dream, Mrs. B. reported concerned New York City, which she thought would be underwater and disappear. She set the singer's death in 1972, the disappearance of New York in May of 1973. Mr. Sinatra is well and hearty and New York City is definitely still above water. To dismiss Mrs. B.'s dreams as publicity-seeking attempts would be unfair and incorrect, however, since she has a good record of psychic accomplishments. But perhaps her conscious self has an interest in Frank Sinatra, or she had read of him at the time of the dreams, and very likely she is familiar with the much publicized Edgar Cayce predictions concerning the inundation of New York City sometime this century. This material, stored in the subconscious, then surfaces again and masquerades as psychic dream material, when in fact it is nothing more than impressions from external sources retold—not genuine psychic communications.

Ruth Kelley is retired, having spent thirty-eight years as a professional librarian in the Boston area. Many years ago she started a dream diary, parts of which she communicated to the Boston Society for Psychical Research, and later to Laura Dale of the American Society for Psychical Research in New York City. Many of her precognitive dreams are of a personal nature, others can be recorded here, especially as they have shown amazingly accurate verifications later on. Here then are her entries in her dream diary.

May 31, 1941, she dreamt that her cat broke his yellow plate. The following day this really happened when the cat slapped the plate while her mistress was serving her breakfast. This is interesting since it proves we can have psychic dreams concerning animals as well as people.

December 18, 1940, Mrs. Kelley dreamt that her neighbor, Edward B., had started a fire on his land, that the fire spread onto her land and the fire department was called out to deal with it. On Easter Sunday, 1941, the event took place. He did start a fire, it crossed over onto her land, and she called the fire department.

A particularly evidential dream occurred to Mrs. Kelley on January 21, 1942. Although the dream was rather vague in details, it was about a certain Ruth Miller. Because she kept a diary, she was able to verify the dream when it did come true in May 1956. At that time Mrs. Kelley was on a train returning from the West. The train was crowded and she happened to sit beside a stranger. A conversation ensued, and the stranger introduced herself by the name of Ruth Miller. She and Mrs. Kelley later corresponded after returning to their respective homes.

About this same time Mrs. Kelley had a dream in which she saw a friend named Isabel, who was wearing a hat with a bunch of blue flowers on it and a blue bow. This dream surprised Mrs. Kelley, since Isabel is a milliner and personally prefers plain, simple hats. It wasn't likely that she would wear such a hat. A short time after the dream, however, she met Isabel wearing precisely such a hat, exactly as she had seen it in her dream. Apparently a friend had given her the hat and since she really didn't like it, she said she would never wear it again.

Sometimes psychic dreams can be incomplete, leaving out details. I do not think that this is due to the dreamer forgetting the details on awakening, but simply cases of incomplete communications.

On November 29, 1942, Mrs. Kelley dreamt of a yellow cat lying in the road, and as a car started the driver held the door open and the cat hopped in. On December 6, 1942, a yellow cat was hit by a car in front of her house and a policeman took it out into her back lot and shot it to stop its suffering. The next day he took the body away in the car.

Other dreams combine two essentially unconnected messages or scenes into one dream, which makes the understanding of such dream material very difficult. On August 26, 1946, Mrs. Kelley dreamt about patients in an institution and that the patients, all children, were in a train wreck. The following day the New York *Times* printed an account of a train wreck that had occurred the night before. The train had been full of children. However, at the time of the dream, Mrs. Kelley was in Albany, New York, and reading Phyllis Bottome's *Lifeline*, which deals with institutions.

I could go on and on with material of this kind, all of it verified, all of it told to witnesses prior to the event taking place in reality. But I think the evidence is overwhelming as it stands. In summing up this category, prophetic dreams, it appears to me that they cannot be forced to occur at will, that they are not directional in the sense other categories of dreams are, but much more haphazard, as if the precognitive contact were made at random, regardless of importance, regardless of the dreamer's own needs or connections. We must therefore seek an explanation for this ability to dream true in the mechanics of dreaming itself. Something occurs in the makeup of the dreamer's personality during sleep which allows his/her unconscious mind to tune in on the future events recorded in the dream. It may be that the area covered by the dreamer is linked to geographical concepts, or to intensity concepts, or to some other form of attraction. For the present, let us be satisfied to state that prophetic dreams are fairly common, cannot be regulated in any way, but can be verified and should, as a matter of fact, always be told on arising to competent witnesses.

WARNING
DREAMS

As I have already pointed out briefly, there is a basic difference between psychic dreams of future events and warning dreams: the psychic dream foresees events that will actually occur, as seen in the dream, whereas a warning dream contains an element of urgency, to do something about the potential outcome of a certain situation. Warning dreams portray scenes precisely the way psychic dreams do, but with the difference that they are portrayed merely as possibilities which may be averted under certain conditions. The tantalizing thing about these warning dreams is that you are never sure whether or not you can in fact avert the outcome of the dream.

As I look at the material accumulated in my files or that I have studied through the years, I find certain characteristics in these warning dreams. For one thing, the overwhelming majority of warning dreams presents a scene in which the dreamer is an onlooker rather than a participant. Even where the dreamer appears in the picture, it is with a clear understanding that this does not actually "happen," and is without the sense of foreboding so common to psychic dreams pertaining to future happenings. Again, from my experience with this type of material, there is a *purpose* in warning dreams, and that is to forewarn the principal or someone known to the principal, of a potential danger, or some other impending event, usually with a degree of severity. It is clear that whoever "sends" these warning dreams intends them to be regarded as just that. Of course, if the dreamer is unaware of the nature of such dream material and chooses to ignore it, the "authority" who has supplied the warning dream is off the hook, so to speak. There seems to be some kind of delicate law of balance in effect here, by which certain people are given warnings of disaster, while others are not so favored. Possibly this may relate to accumulated or earned karma, possibly to other factors unknown to us. It isn't always necessary for a dreamer to realize the warning nature of his/her paranormal dream, either, so long as he/she is generally aware of the possibility of receiving such information through the dream state. In that case, when the dangerous situation begins to come into his/her consciousness, his/her memory will be jagged and the dream warning trigger some sort of preventive action.

A good case in point is a dream which occurred several years ago to my good friend Michael Bentine, an English entertainer and writer. At that time he was traveling to various parts of England as a cabaret performer, frequently going to smaller places in the provinces for the first time. During one season he had a particularly vivid dream, while in London, in which he saw himself in his car driving along a country road which he did not recognize. In his dream he saw himself round a curve, when suddenly there appeared ahead of him the headlights of an oncoming car, traveling at great speed in his direction. Michael did not actually see the crash, but he felt that a crash was imminent as the dream ended. Nevertheless, the dream slipped his memory, as the weeks went by. Toward the end of the season he happened to be in the North Country of England, when one night he found himself driving along unfamiliar roads. As he was about to round a bend in the road, he noticed in the distance the headlights of an oncoming car. At that precise moment, the road seemed suddenly familiar to him, even though he had never traveled on it before. In an instant he recognized it as the strange road of his dream, and the oncoming car as the headlights of his dream car. The recognition of this situation allowed him to take evasive action, just in time to avoid a head-on collision.

Whenever the dreamer finds him/herself in the dream suffering some tragic fate, and feels that the tragedy befalling him/her is real, then I don't think we are dealing with a warning dream but rather with a premonitory experience which will eventually happen to the dreamer. On the other hand, much of the warning dream material is not precise but rather vague, in that one dreams one should not do certain things, or undertake certain journeys, or see a certain person on some particular day. The line between premonitions occurring in the state bordering on sleep and actual warning dreams is sometimes very thin, and there is certainly a connection between the two phenomena. Warning material may also be contained in a different category of dreams which I have termed survival dreams, with which I will deal in a later chapter. In this type dream a discarnate entity, a spirit, as it were, appears or speaks to the dreamer and warns him/her of certain dangers in the future. I have not included such dreams here because they are primarily communication dreams, not images or impressions in which the dreamer him/herself is the primary recipient. Also, the degree to which such dreams are accepted will depend on the dreamer's attitude toward the possibility of spirits communicating with him in the dream state. Unfortunately, many psychiatrists have explained dreams of dead relatives as suppressed emotional hang-ups of one kind or another, not as the actual intercession by those deceased relatives.

Such dreams are not warning dreams in the true sense because they do not permit the dreamer a choice, they either spell it out or actually protect him/her from the coming hurt.

Actress Gloria DeHaven was driving on a road she was not too familiar with, when her deceased mother appeared to her in the windshield of her car, holding up a hand. Immediately Miss DeHaven stopped her car, and the image disappeared. On getting out of the car she found that she was but a few yards away from an abyss. Unknown to her, the road had been washed out.

Here we have an incident which does not permit the percipient to consider the matter; the dead take action, and the action is successful. The incident reported by Gloria DeHaven occurred while she was fully awake, of course, but similar occurrences have been happening to people while asleep, again because it is easier for discarnates to make contact with people in this dimension.

Naturally, as with all psychic material, we must be aware of externalized personal pressures, or material originating in one's own unconscious. It is entirely possible for people with psychoneurotic problems to create false dream material, which is the proper province of psychoanalysts. But such dreams are heavily interlarded with symbolism, are usually extremely confused in content, and contain entire series of images. True warning dreams are nearly always precise and to the point, almost like a Western Union message.

Mrs. Howard Hitt is a housewife and mother in her late twenties, living in northern California. Her husband is a salesman, and they live an average life. The dream in question occurred to Mrs. Hitt during the last week of June 1970. At the time she and her husband were planning a trip to Reno, Nevada. In the dream she became aware of an accident involving two people. Although the two people were not clear enough to identify, Mrs. Hitt had a strong feeling that an infant was involved. On awakening, she remembered the dream, without being able to give exact details concerning the nature of the accident. But the feeling was so strong that she wanted to cancel the trip. On the other hand, she knew that her husband had been looking forward to it, so she did not at first tell him about the dream. However, she decided to leave their six-month-old baby at home with her mother.

All week long she felt uneasy about the trip. "Finally at about eleven P.M. on the night before our Fourth of July trip, as we were resting for it, the feeling was so strong that I decided to mention it to my husband. To my surprise he confessed he also had had some apprehension all week," Mrs. Hitt explained. They decided to go anyway, but to be extremely cautious because of the dream. To their relief they arrived safely in Reno. But on their return trip they had a lot of trouble with their car, and what should have been an easy four-and-a- half-hour trip turned into ten hours. Under the circumstances Mrs. Hitt thought that the dream had simply been a warning that there would be difficulties with their car. But when they reached home, her mother informed her that someone had been trying to reach her by telephone. It turned out that the Hitts' best friends, Mr. and Mrs. Richard B., had been returning from a drive-in movie on July 4, when they were struck by an oncoming car about a block from their home. The car was completely demolished and both friends were injured and hospitalized. Mrs. Hitt now felt that the dream had pertained to her best friends, rather than to herself. On the other hand, how was she to explain the feeling about an infant being involved? Mrs. B. then admitted that they had been thinking of taking the Hitts and the Hitts' children with them to the movie, but on learning later that they were about to leave on a trip to Reno had abandoned this idea.

It is interesting that Mrs. Hitt's dream "tuned in on" the situation as it existed *prior* to the final arrangements being made just before the trip itself. But because the dreamer was unable to identify the couple in the dream, she was not in a position to relate it to the proper individuals, and thus take preventive action.

There is no satisfactory explanation why some ordinary people dream about celebrities with whom they have absolutely no connection, not even as fans. The fate of famous people is no different from that of the unknown amongst us, yet there are instances where average people dream of well-known actors or other people in the limelight, without being in a position of doing anything about their prophetic dreams.

Louise S. is a housewife in her middle thirties, happily married and the mother of three children. She is interested in ESP and psychical research and has read a great deal about the subject. She makes her home in a small town in

Ohio. On January 23, 1969, she dreamt that Bobby Darin had very serious heart disease. It came to her almost like a message, but it puzzled her since she had had no special interest in the singer's life. Nor had she read or heard anything about him immediately before the dream. Curiously enough, precisely two years to the day after this dream she was listening to the radio when she heard in the news that Bobby Darin had just had serious heart surgery. Darin passed away of his heart ailment in 1973. Mrs. S.'s prophetic dream was registered with me on March 4, 1971.

Frequently, pregnant women are unusually sensitive to psychic communication and intuition. Mrs. Marjorie F. lived in Illinois at the time she registered this dream material with me in May of 1974. She has a bachelor's degree in elementary education, and is married to an officer in the United States Air Force. In May 1969, she was pregnant with her third child. At that time she had a dream that a boy would be born to her but that he would not live. On May 31, 1969, she became the mother of a son, born three months prematurely. Despite an early negative prognosis, the child picked up in health and gained weight. Three weeks after his birth, all seemed well for the premature baby, so much so that a photographer was called in to take pictures. But on the thirtieth day of his life, the baby died suddenly, just as she had foreseen in her dream.

Mrs. Jean M. is fifty-one, a widow with four children, living in Nova Scotia. She used to work as a bank clerk, until her marriage to an air force officer. All her life she remembers having had veridical dreams, but feared to mention some of them because of prevailing prejudices. In March 1959 her husband was sent on a course at Saskatoon, while stationed in Chatham, New Brunswick. A few nights after he had left Mrs. M. had a terrible nightmare. In it she saw herself and her children standing around a casket, crying. Next she saw herself in a car with a hearse ahead of her and the air force guard of honor marching. The dream was so vivid that she was sure something had happened to her husband and she was understandably on edge until he returned home safely. Then the memory of her dream gradually faded, and eventually she decided that it had been nothing more than a bad dream. But in November of the same year, he suddenly died from a heart attack. As a result of this tragedy, she found herself in a car behind a hearse, and the honor guard marched precisely as it had in her dream, eight months before.

Not all warning dreams are as tragic in their consequences. Denise Shamlian of San Francisco, California is an artist by profession, has an IQ of 155, and is in her very early thirties. In January 1972 she moved to Paris. There she had occasion to see a dentist named Dr. Jean-Claude W., one of the most prominent dentists in Paris at the time. He gave her a gold inlay. Three nights before she left Paris, she had a vivid dream in which she saw the inlay halfway out of her tooth, and causing her a lot of pain. The following day she mentioned this to a friend, who laughed at her because the inlay seemed in fine shape and the dentist had a brilliant reputation. Dismissing her dream fears, Miss Shamlian returned to San Francisco. The night before Easter 1972 she woke up with a toothache due to the inlay being halfway out. It was exactly as it had come to her in the dream in Paris.

Robert P. B. was a captain in the United States Air Force when he registered one of his wife's dreams with me on July 26, 1971. He has since left the Air Force and holds a Bachelor of Science degree in microbiology. His wife, Nina, studied at the University of Southern California extension in Munich, Germany, while they were stationed there. It was in Munich that Mrs. B. had the following vivid dream. On July 11, 1968, she saw herself with a black eye; furthermore, she received the impression that a good friend of hers named Jeannie, also would have a blackened eye received in connection with the terrace of her third-floor dormitory room. The following morning, Mrs. B. related the dream to Jeannie and advised her to stay away from her terrace. But her warning was ignored, and the following Saturday night, July 13, Jeannie went to a dance at one of the local servicemen's clubs in Munich. She returned to the dormitory by curfew time, about 10:30 P.M. During the course of the evening she had had a disagreement with her boyfriend, and about midnight she decided to sneak out of the dormitory to try and make up with him. She did this by tying a rope to the terrace of her room and trying to slide down to the ground. In the attempt, however, she slipped and fell three stories. She received various injuries, including two blackened eyes. She then remembered the warning given her by Mrs. B. and blamed her, in some strange fashion, for the incident, thus giving Nina a "spiritual" black eye as well.

Mrs. June L. works for a large bank in upstate New York and her husband is a salesman. They are grandparents several times over. Her premonitory experiences are partially in the form of waking impressions, partially in the form of dreams. Sometime in late October 1948, when her third son, Dick, was two years old, she had a frightening dream in which she saw her son crying with pain in his hip and blood gushing from it. It made no sense to her at all at the time, but several months later her son began to drag his right foot and cry. The doctor established that the boy was suffering from a lack of Vitamin C and was bleeding internally from the hip. The child was immediately cured, but had the dream been properly understood, he might have been saved some of the suffering.

Mrs. Sue T. still wants to develop her innate ESP ability, despite some harrowing experiences with psychic dreams. The attractive young woman is a professional model, thirty years old, and lives with her husband and children in Pennsylvania. The first dream she ever had seemed silly to her. She was in her bathroom trying to remove a splinter from her finger. Suddenly she remembered a dream she had had that afternoon, in which she saw herself pricking her finger just as her mother- and father-in-law came to the door of the bathroom. She had barely thought about this when her in-laws appeared at the door just as she had dreamt.

But her next dream was not as silly to her, and turned out to be a nightmare in the end.

She and her husband had moved into a new house, and had had their second and third child. At that time she had a very strange dream, from which she awoke crying. In her dream she had had an apartment of her own, and several children, when there was a knock at her door and outside stood her husband saying, "I want you to meet my wife." There was a strange woman with him but Mrs. T. could not remember what she looked like. She reported the dream to her husband, remarking how silly it all seemed to her.

A short time later her husband was transferred to a small town in Pennsylvania. Somehow this began to destroy their marriage, and the difficult times she went through made her forget the strange dream she had had before they moved. Then she had another unusual dream. In this one she saw herself walking from their living room into the bedroom and when she opened the door she could see the kitchen table from the door. There sat her husband with a man she had never seen before. At this instant a thought flashed through her mind that the man was someone who was supposed to kill her, on her husband's instigation. With this she awoke screaming.

About that time her marriage came to an end and she left her husband in March 1971. Late in October 1972, her ex-husband was supposed to have brought a car down to show her and she was therefore expecting him. When he arrived at her house, a young woman was with him whom Mrs. T. recognized as the woman in her first dream. However, he did not introduce her as his wife, even though the implication as to her relationship with him was clear. After this, relations between Mrs. T. and her ex-husband became worse, and there were arguments over some property. She realized that her ex-husband had a key to her apartment, and remembering her second dream, she lived in constant fear of him. Eventually, she moved away to be safe.

Mrs. S. G. has eight grandchildren, but still works as a law secretary in the eastern United States. During World War II she and her husband had bought a number of United States bonds but had difficulty finding a safe-deposit box for their safekeeping. Her husband mentioned that his employer would keep the bonds in the company safe for them. A few years went by and then one night she dreamt that two thieves broke the skylight in the building, blew up the safe and took out all the contents. She told her husband about the dream and insisted that he take out the bonds, but he only laughed at her. The following night, she had the identical dream, and this time she made such a fuss over it that on the Friday of the same week he asked his employer for the bonds. The following Monday, her husband returned from work and informed his wife that her dream had come true during the weekend. When he asked for his bonds back, Mr. G.'s employer had asked why, but instead of telling him about his wife's premonitory dream (thus possibly preventing the burglary), he made some vague excuse, and let the matter pass.

Miss T. L. of Long Island, New York is an artist by profession. When her ex-husband was in the Army, he frequently stayed away from home for weeks on temporary duty assignments. One night she had a dream in which she saw her ex-husband driving in the mountains. There was heavy snow everywhere. Suddenly she saw an avalanche come down and the car was buried in it. The dream woke her up. At the time her husband was in Utah, so she decided to wait until he would telephone her Sunday night. She mentioned the dream to him and there was a pause on the telephone, then he replied that he had gone up to a ski area, when an avalanche came down the mountainside. It just missed his car but buried the one behind him.

"When I dream of future events that later come true, the dream is always accompanied by a strange feeling of knowing it is not just another ordinary dream," Margaret B. stated, even though her husband ridicules her psychic dreams and considers her superstitious. Mrs. B. has been active on behalf of certain American Indian groups, taking up their cause against injustice. She and her husband and their small girl live in upstate New York. However, at the time of the following dream they were living in Arizona.

Mrs. B. dreamt she was lying on her bed and it was dusk. She heard a shot from the general area of the guesthouse, sprang from her bed and raced downhill to the guesthouse, where she saw two men. One seemed to be her husband lying face down alongside the building; the other was standing on the hill above, watching over the scene. The little light left in the sky allowed her to see only that he was tall and thin, definitely not built like a Yaqui Indian, the people whose cause she and her husband were then furthering. The stranger held a long gun in his hand, with the stock on the ground. She looked hard, but could not make out his face. Then she continued to run to where her husband was. When she reached him, she felt that he was dead, but when she pulled at his shoulders, to turn him over, she realized that he was still alive. Immediately she thought that if the man on the hill realized this, he would shoot again and it was better to pretend that her husband was dead. She told her husband, and looked again at the man on the hill, wondering whether he would shoot at her also. At that moment she woke up. Despite her husband's negative reaction to the dream, she was terrified and insisted that he not go near the guesthouse at any time.

About that time pressure against her husband, herself, and the members of the committee favoring the cause of the Indians mounted. Attempts at arson and attempted murder came with increasing frequency, and, convinced that the dream had been a warning for what was in store for her husband, she insisted that they leave the house and area. In the end, her husband gave in and they left. Here we have a warning dream heeded, with the likelihood of it coming true very great indeed.

Mary C., a native of Arkansas, worked as a waitress until she got married and settled down as a housewife with two children. When her son was seventeen, he owned a 1963 Austin Healy. On March 14, 1973, Mrs. C. had a dream in which she could see the car going from one side of the road to the other. Suddenly, it was smashed up. There was a girl in her dream whom she did not know. Immediately on awakening, she informed her son of her dream, but he would not accept it as meaning anything of substance. Several days later, the boy decided to pay a call on a girl friend, and since he insisted on it, Mrs. C. let him go. However, the boy promised to telephone as soon as he got to his girl friend's house. A short time later a telephone call came, but it was to advise her that there had been an accident. When Mrs. C. reached the scene of the accident, it looked exactly the way it had looked in her dream several days before. The girl, whom she did not recognize in her dream, was a nurse who had been passing in her car, stopped by and looked after her son. Here we have a warning dream that could have been heeded, but was not.

Mrs. Jeani Magee of Louisiana has had remarkable incidents of ESP practically all her life. But the warning dream she will never forget occurred to her at five in the morning of July 16, 1973. She woke up her husband to tell him of the dream in which she saw a man being shot. Since she did not know who he was, she went back to sleep, remarking, "I don't know what is going to happen to me." She awoke again at eight-thirty, and asked her husband not to go to work that day, which would have been easy since his secretary was on vacation. Her husband promised that he would go to the office only to open his mail and return at noon. It was 10:15 when he left the house. The only people left in the house were Mrs. Magee, the housemaid, the Magees' nine-year-old daughter, Cathy, and their ten-month-old daughter, Ashley. What transpired fifteen minutes after her husband left the house was reported by the Associated Press as follows:

"A kidnaper who held off Sheriff's deputies by pointing a gun at a 10-month-old baby's head was shot in the back and killed at a roadblock on Monday when he turned to shoot at officers. About 10:45 A.M. two men broke into the Magees' home, tied Mrs. Magee with rope, robbed the house and fled with about $400 in cash, Magee's car and the girl. A neighbor called the police and officers quickly spotted the big white Cadillac in which the men fled."

After the chase, the child was recovered without injury and returned to her parents, but no description can sufficiently reflect the horror Mrs. Magee went through when her baby was taken by the bandits. Had her husband heeded his wife's warning and not gone to the office to look after his mail, perhaps things would have come out differently, perhaps not.

The next dream may be a plain warning dream, or it may be due to the indirect action by a discarnate friend, trying to make what was to come easier to bear. At any rate, Mrs. Sue P. of California dreamt in 1967 that her son and she were in a large gathering. Her husband was with them, but all of a sudden he disappeared, and Mrs. P. told her son to look for his father. Shortly afterward the son returned crying, saying his father was dead. The following morning she related this dream to her husband, Dr. C. P. The doctor laughed, and dismissed it as "only a dream." He was in perfect health, and there was no reason for alarm. Several weeks later, Mrs. P. had another dream. In this one she saw herself scanning a local newspaper, when she turned to the obituaries. There she saw her husband's name among those who had died, plain as day. The dream frightened her, especially as it recurred a week later. The following week, Doctor C. P. died suddenly from a heart attack.

Could the doctor's acceptance of the warning dream have prevented his demise at that point? Assuming that he took his wife's dream seriously, he might have undergone special testing, and perhaps discovered some indication of a pending heart attack. Was the dream "sent" to Mrs. P. by "the authorities" beyond this world to give the doctor an even chance to do something about his imminent death? Is this a case where free will enters the picture, that is, the action undertaken by the individual having drastic bearing on the outcome? Or was the doctor on "the list," regardless of his reaction to his wife's premonitory dream. Clearly, we cannot be sure in this case, since the event took place as foreseen.

Lastly, there are seemingly valid warning dreams resembling those that actually come true later, except they haven't come true as dreamt. Such material may either be "false" dream material caused by personal fears of the dreamer.

or it may be simply dream material, still pertaining to the future. We do not know, therefore, whether the dream was in fact a warning dream or not.

An interesting and rather typical case of this kind is a warning dream reported to me by Mrs. Carol C. of Huntington Beach, California. She is a housewife with two children, in her early thirties, and living in a lovely house on the beach. She doesn't consider herself psychic, although she has had a few things happen to her which "surprised her." She admits having a vivid imagination, and a lively interest in the predictions of others, is well read in ESP material, and aware of the many predictions made about earthquakes and tidal waves in California. Nevertheless, she reported a dream in which she saw a tidal wave come onto a beach where she found herself with her children. There were other people there also when the huge wave came in, and she could feel rock walls around her buckle and crumble, but somehow she and her children were not hurt.

To my knowledge, the dream has not yet become objective reality, as no large tidal wave has been reported hitting Huntington Beach. Was the dream the result of general, deep-seated fears concerning natural catastrophes involving the California coastline, or was it a specific, individual dream pertaining to a situation that may yet come true?

I hesitated to include the next dream in this chapter because it concerns a well-known personality and has not yet come true, may, in fact, never come true. On the other hand, if it does by the inscrutable will of fate actually happen, recording it here would help in understanding the phenomena involved, so I have decided to include it.

Under a postmark of June 1969, a woman named Shirley Griffith, who lives in Texas, registered a strange dream with me. It has upset her greatly, as does the question of committing it to public print, but she wanted me to have the contents as a matter of record.

Sunday night, June 15, 1969, around 3 A.M., she dreamt of an auto accident on a lonely country road which had a barbed wire fence running along one side of it. On that side the field was higher than the road and it kept ascending at a gentle slant to a low hill. The grass was tall and golden, with the light resembling late afternoon. On top of the hill she saw a clump of dark green bushes, very full in foliage. The car involved was low-slung and built for speed, and she kept thinking that it was a Jaguar and of the color red. Only one person was involved, and the accident was due to too much speed, there was a bright flash and only bits and pieces of the car were left rolling down the road in a huge fireball. Almost instantly, a newspaper clipping appeared in her dream. The picture of the man in the newspaper story was that of an actor, W. S. The newspaper headline was about three quarters of an inch high, heavy and black, with the picture on the left and three columns of small type to the right, all evenly spaced. The story thus was wider than it was long. She distinctly remembered feeling the physical shock of this man's death and she remembers crying in her sleep. The dream of the accident seemed steady and, except for the above mentioned action, it did not move. But with the appearance of the newspaper clipping it started to recede, at first slowly, then more rapidly, until she woke up with a gasp.

As soon as she had gathered her wits, Griffith told her mother about the dream. Now, Griffith, neither knows the actor, nor has she been interested in knowing him; but she admits to personal feelings about the star. This, of course, makes her reluctant to accept the dream as valid, since it might be due to her romantic fantasy about the actor. On the other hand, the intensity of the dream seems to indicate something more than a fan's imagination. Only the future will tell which it was.

ESP DREAMS

The term ESP dreams may surprise some who are used to other terms, but I have chosen the term because I am covering here three types of dream material with one thing in common—they do in no way pertain to the future.

ESP dreams are first of all *telepathic dreams*, in which the dreamer perceives or receives messages or information from another person, either living or dead, but pertaining to the present, even if at a distance. In telepathic dreams, the transmission need not be conscious, or exact. The dreamer simply picks up thought energies. Both *contemplated* events and actual events may be the subject for such dreams.

Somewhat different is the second type of ESP dreams, *simultaneous dreams*, in which the dreamer tunes in on an event going on at a distance. In simultaneous dreams, the dreamer is present without being seen, seemingly extending part of his consciousness beyond the barriers of space and without regard to distance or solid objects in between. Those dreams where the dreamer is also noticed at a distant location from his physical whereabouts are not dreams at all, but are part of the phenomenon called out-of-the-body experience, with which I will deal in a subsequent chapter.

Finally, there is the dream category called *retrocognitive dreams*, in which the dreamer relives an event that has already taken place in the past, but with which he/she is not familiar in his/her conscious state. Retrocognitive dreams somewhat resemble psychometry experiments, in which a psychic person touches an object and reconstructs the object's past merely from this contact. But with retrocognitive dreams, the dreamer does not have a choice of direction. Usually, the dream is unexpected and does not necessarily require the physical presence of the dreamer in a location to which the dream material refers. ESP dreams, then, are simply extensions of ordinary consciousness, and they afford the dreamer insight into events or situations which with he/she would not normally be familiar at the time of their occurrences.

We should, of course, be careful not to label dreams that are clearly symbolic or of psychoanalytical value as ESP dreams. What I've said before pertaining to the difference between psychic dreams in general and those more suitable for psychoanalytical interpretation, is particularly important here, where we do not have an element of prophecy but are dealing with contemporary or past matters, the latter having already occurred and therefore at least theoretically capable of being picked up consciously by the dreamer. But the clarity of the ESP dream and its strong remembrance upon awakening sets it apart from the dream material suitable for psychoanalytical interpretation. A trained observer will know the difference.

Mrs. J. W. of New Jersey had a dream experience which comes under this heading. In 1941 a very close friend of hers was serving aboard an oil tanker which was then based at Fort Pierce, Florida. The tanker was torpedoed by a German submarine while at sea and all but one of the crew perished. At that time, Mrs. W. had a vivid dream in which she saw her friend trapped in his room. He was pounding the door with his fists and she was able to notice a porcelain doorknob which he kept bearing down on. All the time he kept crying out for her, calling her by his pet name for her, over and over; at this point the dream ended. Several hours later she was notified that he had died in the attack on the tanker.

It would appear that the dream coincided with the actual moment of her friend's death and that in his anxiety he had called out to the strongest emotional tie he then had, reaching her across the miles while asleep. Obviously, the doomed man must have known that his friend could not help him where he was, but perhaps he wanted her to know that she was the last thing on his mind, or perhaps he simply acted in panic, when rationalization is usually absent.

Mrs. A. W. is a Canadian, now living in Massachusetts. She has two sons and a daughter. When she contacted me, she was working as a statistical typist in a bank. Mrs. W. has had many psychic experiences throughout her career. One of the first ones, however, is of interest here since it belongs in the category I am discussing.

At the time she was eight years old she had great difficulty understanding long division. She thought she was the only one in her class who couldn't grasp it; her teacher was exasperated because of her lack of comprehension. When she tried to get aid from her classmates it didn't help at all since she couldn't understand their explanations either. She then turned to her sister to learn the intricacies of the subject, but received little solace there. One night, worried over her incomprehension, she prayed for help with her vexing problem, and went to bed. That night she had a most enlightening dream. She saw herself back in the schoolroom. Her teacher summoned her to the blackboard, where she was confronted with three problems in long division. In the dream, Mrs. W. picked up the chalk and proceeded to solve the problems effortlessly and correctly.

The following morning Mrs. W. went to school as usual. In class, the teacher summoned her to the blackboard. Three problems in long division confronted her, exactly as they had in her dream, and just as she had dreamt it, she proceeded to solve them correctly and effortlessly.

Now, on the surface of it, this dream pertains to the future and should therefore be listed among

the examples in my chapter on prophetic dreams.
But this is not so; the ability to solve long division
was buried in Mrs. W.'s unconscious, present but
unrealized. Surely, her teacher had selected the
next day's assignment when going to bed that
night. What the girl dreamt then was of a dual
nature; on the one hand, she was tuning in on her
teacher's thoughts, obtaining a simultaneous view
of the problems she would be confronted with the
following day, and on the other hand, she was
unlocking her own unconscious as a reassuring
step to help her with the next day's work.

Mrs. Catherine H. is a housewife in her early
forties who lives in Pennsylvania. Her entire
family, consisting of husband and three daughters, is extremely telepathic, so she has no
problems being recognized in this area. She has
had precognitive dreams for many years, in fact,
she says, too numerous to list. "I have precognitive
dreams which are sifted from the rest by the
presence of the color green somewhere in the
dream," she explains. One particularly impressive
dream she reported to me under the postmark of
February 8, 1971. In the dream she saw green
mountains, and several trucks sinking into black
slime which was covering the entire mountain.
She saw the trucks and suddenly found *herself*
trapped very deeply under the trucks and some
wood. She heard herself scream until she almost
lost her voice. At that moment someone called out

to her, warning her that she would lose her voice. That was the end of the dream.

Two weeks later, the great tragedy at Aberfan, Great Britain, shook the world: a coal slag slide buried a schoolhouse killing many children. The newspaper story, which reached Mrs. H. two weeks *after* her dream, stated among other harrowing experiences, that a worker heard a child screaming because she was trapped under the rubble. The worker called out to the child to stop screaming and asked for her name, to which she replied, Catherine. "Most experiences become a reality about two weeks after I dream them and most of them pertain to world disasters," Mrs. H. explained. "I also feel the pain of a stricken person for the tragedy." Because of this unwanted talent, she consulted a medical doctor, hoping that he would rid her of it. But the reality of her psychic ability has remained with her.

Now, Mrs. H. is by no means the only one who has somehow tuned in on the Aberfan disaster. A London newspaper investigated the prophetic dreams of many who foresaw it and described it in accurate detail. What makes this particular dream different from all the others and incidentally the reason why I am reporting it here in my chapter on ESP dreams and not with other prophetic dreams, is Mrs. H.'s personal identification with another individual. Mrs. H. does not merely dream of an event in the future, seeing people at a distance of whom she knows nothing. In this case, at least, she became the child trapped under the truck. There is no easy way of explaining how this was possible. If the event itself was already slated at the time Mrs. H. had the dream, the reaction of the trapped girl could not have very well been. Also, Mrs. H. makes much of the identity of the names, she and the stricken girl both being Catherine. But the dream, more than anything else, seems to me to contain a key to the better understanding of the time-space continuum in which we live, and permits me to offer the tantalizing suggestion—far from making it a theory—how such dreams are indeed possible. What if our realistic experiencing of events was somehow a *delayed* realization of the events, while the events themselves take place *earlier* without our being aware of them until later? Those who have psychically foreseen such events are then not looking into the future but are able to pick up the *present* when it happens, while the majority of us are not. This, of course, is merely idle speculation.

Mrs. C. is a third-grade schoolteacher who lives in Indiana and who has five daughters and one son. One of these daughters, Laverne, is a housewife and works as a part-time practical nurse at a local hospital. She had never believed in the reality of psychic phenomena until her mother had a certain dream. It happened in 1967, when the daughter was five months pregnant. Laverne went into labor and had to be taken to the hospital at one o'clock in the morning. Medical authorities said she would lose the baby and at 2 A.M. her husband was sent home. At 3 A.M. Laverne woke up and began to cry, "Dear God, please help me, I want my mother." She repeated it several times until she drifted back to sleep. Although she had been married for five years she had never felt so much in need of her mother, but she also knew that her mother couldn't come to her aid since her mother was then living in Indiana.

When next she saw her mother, four months later, her mother informed her of a strange dream she had had at the same time Laverne had been in the hospital. At 3 A.M. her mother had dreamt that she was in a bedroom downstairs in the house belonging to another daughter. In the dream she had turned the bedroom light off and started upstairs when she heard her daughter call for her. She turned back into the bedroom. There was a bright light coming from a corner where her daughter lay on a flat board or stretcher. She was wearing a pale blue gown. Since Mrs. C. had five daughters she was not sure which daughter this was, but assumed it was Laverne's older sister, since the dream occurred in that sister's house. She went upstairs, where she found her son sitting on the sofa, and begged him to come downstairs to see what was wrong with his sister. He refused to go and kept saying not to worry because everything would be all right. Finally, the mother became angry and turned to go downstairs alone, but the light had faded and the daughter on the stretcher was now gone.

Mrs. C.'s dream was so vivid that it woke her up, and she began to pray for Laverne's older sister. At the time that sister was in Africa as a missionary and the mother quite naturally assumed that she was in some sort of danger since the dream had taken place in her home.

The following morning the mother was informed that Laverne had lost her baby and it was then that she thought about her dream. It occurred to her that the sister in Africa always wore pajamas, while Laverne usually preferred gowns. Also, she remembered that the last time Laverne had visited with her sister and mother, who were then living together, she had slept in the downstairs bedroom and had worn a pale blue gown.

What we have here is a simultaneous dream in which the mother was able to tune in on her daughter's condition, hearing her cries for help but somehow intermingling this direct telepathic material with unconscious knowledge of her daughter's appearance the last time she had actually been at the house of the dream. In this case, the dreamer, unconsciously of course, draws upon earlier accumulated dream knowledge and uses it to "flesh out," as it were, the new dream in which telepathic material is received.

Simultaneous psychic dreams generally relate to events taking place at exactly the same moment, although at a distance, which can range anywhere from the house next door to some location clear across the country. Occasionally, simultaneous dreams allow for time differences so that the dreamer gets the impression at the time the event occurs in its own time zone, but at a different time where the dreamer lives.

I also consider simultaneous ESP dreams those where events occur within a few hours before the dream takes place but without the dreamer's knowledge of the event. For instance, an event may take place in the dead of night, but it comes to the dreamer's attention only when he/she wakes the next morning. At that time the dreamer is able to confirm his/her dream of the night before, even though, technically speaking, he/she dreamt of it *afterward*. In the same way, I also consider dreams becoming objective reality *slightly* later than dreamt as part of this category, pointing out the need to re-appraise our concepts of time. Perhaps time is not as absolute as we think, but is capable of flexibility. All this remains to be worked out by future observation and experiments.

Mrs. Dorothy T. lives in northern California. She is a housewife and has several children. Brought up a strict Roman Catholic, her psychic gift was suppressed in boarding school, but was allowed to develop freely later on in life. Although she lived hundreds of miles away, she saw, in a dream, her son being brushed by a car in San Francisco. She saw not only a car, but also her mother-in-law being hurt, although not badly. Immediately upon awakening from the dream, she went next door to tell her neighbor. Two days later there was a telephone call informing her that the accident had indeed taken place as she had seen it, but that neither victim was seriously hurt.

Perhaps the most astonishing psychic dream Mrs. T. recorded with me concerned the assassination of President Kennedy. Lee Harvey Oswald had been arrested and the day's events had been most upsetting when Mrs. T. went to bed that night. She had dreamt of a conversation between two people, someone saying, "We will get him in the stomach, it is a painful death," and this woke her up. She immediately told her husband that Oswald was dead by shooting and before her husband could reply, she went into the living room and turned on the television set; the scene was *just then* happening before her eyes!

Not every true dreamer is happy at having the power. "My problem concerns the fact that I get feelings or dream about things before they happen. Unfortunately they are not always good," Jan S. of Maryland complained to me.

In 1968, when Jan was a junior in high school, a boy she knew would always pick her up at school. On this particular day another boy, named Ronnie, came with him. Jan had not seen Ronnie for at least three months prior and the conversation was an ordinary one. That night she had a dream about a boy who shot himself, but unfortunately she could not make out a face; however, she knew it was a friend. The next day when she came to school she found out that Ronnie had shot himself during the night.

Jane Duke is a tremendously gifted psychic woman living in Bakersfield, California. She was able to foresee her first husband's death and prepare for it, as well as many other events in her life to the point where she can program herself to dream of a certain problem and frequently gets answers to her questions. At present, she works as a professional palmist, using this method as an induction agent for her wider psychic talents.

Not long ago a certain young woman whom she did not know previously, came to visit her for a palm reading. Shortly before the arrival of her client, Duke took a nap and dreamt of the problem her client would have on her mind. While she dreamt it, she did not realize that the dream was about her next client, however, but realized it only when she saw her. In the dream, she saw a man who strongly resembled a well-known motion-picture actor. The man put his hand out to her and she looked at it. From it she judged that he was not a good person. Next, in the dream, she saw a dark-haired girl being taken by the hand by this man and led into an elevator, which went down. Duke interpreted this as being a negative situation for the girl. Shortly after she woke up, her client arrived and turned out to be the girl she had seen in the dream. Mrs. Duke went on to describe the man she had seen in the dream and it turned out that he was the reason for the girl's visit to her. Mrs. Duke warned her about him, describing the dream. But the girl would not listen and married the man. Two weeks after marrying him, he beat her up very badly and she left him.

An interesting incident of retrocognitive dreaming occurred to Claudia Cunningham of Pennsylvania, who is an artist by profession.

A friend, Mrs. Emma Black, owned a farmhouse in eastern Pennsylvania which she had made available as a guesthouse to visiting artists. Not long ago, Cunningham stayed there for a few days. That particular week there were six women staying at the guesthouse, two to a room. Cunningham's roommate had gone into the big bedroom across the hall to play cards with the others who were not yet ready to go to sleep. They were talking and laughing as Cunningham undressed and opened the window by her bed. She set the alarm clock and lay down. As she started to relax, ready to drift into sleep, she still heard the voices across the hall. At the threshold of sleep she saw superimposed on the room in which she lay an older, shabbier room with stained wallpaper, poorly furnished and drab. A woman was sitting on a straight chair and leaning her arms against the windowsill. She had long, dark hair hanging over her shoulders and she was weeping in a heartbroken way. Cunningham could hear her sobs over the fainter sounds of the chatter from the other room. Then there was the sound of feet running down the stairs and the back door slamming. Gradually the woman in the room faded away and only Cunningham's room remained. The sound of the other guests' voices across the hall increased to the usual level. At this point Cunningham drifted into deep sleep, still wondering about her experience.

The following morning, at breakfast, she discussed her experience with her hostess and the others. Mrs. Black confirmed the fact that the room in which Cunningham had slept had indeed belonged to the dark-haired woman she had described, and that the woman had had a great deal of grief because of a retarded child. However, the woman in question was still very much alive and living in a nearby town. What Cunningham had experienced was a dream-like state or perhaps a light dream in which she went back into a previous period of the house and relived a scene from the past. It is interesting to note here that it does not seem to make any difference whether the scene concerns living people or deceased individuals, the psychic essence being one and the same kind.

OUT-OF-THE-BODY EXPERIENCES

Until a few years ago, the peculiar experience of being somewhere else without one's physical body was called astral projection, but more recently it has been referred to as out-of-the-body experiences. The classical work dealing with these phenomena, which are very common, is still Dr. Hereward Carrington and Sylvan Muldoon's book on astral projections, in which Muldoon did the dreaming and Dr. Carrington the reporting.

Robert Monroe, a reputable scientist and electrical engineer with a background in radio, has recorded his own amazing experiences in this field in a highly recommended book entitled *Journeys Out of the Body*. In an earlier work, *ESP and You*, I referred to these experiences somewhat facetiously as "going places without a body," meaning that they are experiences in which the conscious part of self leaves the physical shell and travels, observes and remembers. Essentially, astral travel consists of projection of the inner body or etheric self from the physical body, usually during sleep, but not exclusively so. Astral projections have occurred in the waking condition and are usually referred to as "momentary displacements." However, projections of any length are nearly always part of the dream experience. In this phenomenon the sleeper travels various distances, from just to the ceiling of a room to the other side of the continent, and remains connected with the physical self by a silver cord which is not always visible.

In essence, astral projection can be accomplished in two ways: one, willfully projecting the inner self to a predetermined location and reporting back for purposes of research or information; two, and far more common, involuntary dissociation of the inner self during sleep and travel to external locations. Many or all of the events observed or experienced in the astral state are remembered upon awakening with the same intensity and vivid clarity typical of all true psychic dreams.

Astral projections belong among psychic dreams because they partake of the essential characteristics of all psychic dreams: observation by the dreamer of material or situations unknown in his/her conscious state, disregard for conventional time and space, and ability to recall the experiences upon awakening with impressive clarity. Out-of-the-body (OOB) experiences are, in fact, the opposite of prophetic dreams and, to a lesser degree, of ESP dreams. In the latter categories external material is partaken of by the dreamer, whereas with OOB dreams the dreamer goes outside his/her physical environment to observe for him/herself and upon returning remembers what he/she has seen or experienced. In addition, there is a fourth element which other psychic dreams are not capable of producing: the occasional observation of the dreamer's inner self by outside observers, usually while fully awake.

But it is not with the experimentally induced OOB state I am concerned in this book, since it belongs more properly among trance and other hypnotically induced states of altered consciousness. (Such experiments, I must add, should only be undertaken by fully experienced individuals and under the direction and supervision of trained parapsychologists. They are not a parlor game, and like other states of dissociation of personality, involve certain risks, especially if the subject has health or emotional instability problems.)

What we are concerned with here are spontaneous, unsought astral projections in the dream state, in which the dreamer has no choice or control over his travels. I have said earlier that such travels are extremely common, and that many people ascribe to dreams what is in fact an astral projection. More than one projection can occur in a single night, of course, just as a large number of dreams are possible within the span of one sleep period, as Dr. Stanley Krippner has proven through his rapid eye movement (REM) experiments at the Maimonides (Dream Laboratory) in Brooklyn, New York. It is true that some astral projections are hard to distinguish from ordinary dreams because the dreamer may not always be aware of his travel movements and simply remembers the image or content of the dream, not the technique of dreaming itself. On the other hand, there are many dreams on record where the subject reports several telltale characteristics which immediately classify such dream material as being of out-of-the-body experience type.

Here are the common physical and emotional effects of astral projection.

1. A feeling of extreme fatigue upon awakening, even though one may have slept for many hours more than usual.

2. At the very end of each astral projection, a sensation of falling down from great heights, spinning down to earth, usually coupled with a fear of falling. This represents nothing more than the physical reaction to the "stepping down" of vibrations from the very fast astral projection speed to the much slower movement of the physical body, as the inner self re-enters the physical shell, connects with it and assumes its slower forward speed.

3. A vivid recollection of having gone through seemingly solid walls, or of having seen one's own body below, usually at the beginning of the trip. Sensations of drifting away from the body, at first slowly, rising toward the ceiling of the room, then assuming speed and moving rapidly and sometimes at lightning speed across the landscape, all the time observing the physical landmarks around oneself, and sometimes being conscious of temperature comforts or discomforts, such as chills, moisture or heat. Occasionally, observation

of a shimmering silver cord trailing behind oneself, which is reeled in upon returning.

4. At the end of the journey, or at the destination point, observation of people or scenes, usually without being able to make voice contact. On occasion, visual contact has been recorded.

5. Full possession of one's reasoning faculties, i.e., when observing otherwise familiar scenes one notices anything different or unusual about them.

I have already mentioned Jane Duke of Bakersfield, California in the previous chapter. Shortly before leaving for the East in 1970, Duke dreamt that she was at home in her parents' bedroom. It was early in the morning and her father was just getting up. He looked up and saw her standing there, and said, "What in the hell are you doing here?" Then he went on to the other room. On awakening, Duke recorded the dream.

Two weeks later she actually went East to stay with her parents. At first she did not mention anything about her dream because she knew her parents did not believe in such things and had no interest in the occult. But one day her father took her aside and mentioned that he had seen her standing in their bedroom one morning not long ago, when he knew good and well that she was in California. He said he was so startled when he saw her standing there, that all he could say was, "What in the hell are you doing here?" He had mentioned this experience to his wife at the time it occurred. Duke had actually been seen cross-country in Pennsylvania while she was asleep in Bakersfield, California.

On another occasion, when she was again planning to leave for the East, she had a dream in which she was back home. She saw her father and mother out in the yard, hanging up clothes. She tried to talk to them but they didn't notice her at all and went on about their business as though she wasn't there. It occurred to Duke that it was very odd for her parents to be hanging clothes on the line because they had a washer and dryer and should have had no need to hang out their clothes. The following week Duke arrived at her parents' house in Pennsylvania. Shortly after her arrival, her mother mentioned that their dryer had been broken for the past three weeks and they had to wait for a replacement part for it before it could be fixed. But in the meantime she and Duke's father had been hanging the clothes out on the line.

Elaine F. of Pennsylvania has been mentioned in one of the previous chapters. She has come by her psychic talents through inheritance, it would appear, because her mother has recorded a most amazing out-of-the-body experience. In this particular dream she returned to a town she had been to before in similar dreams. The sun was shining brightly and she met a man she had never seen before and found herself talking to him. He then handed her his sunglasses and she heard herself say something about giving them back to him because he would need them. He advised her that he would be back for them.

The next day, Elaine F. and her mother went shopping. When her mother went to get her coat—the same coat she had been wearing in the dream the night before—she found a pair of men's sunglasses in one of the pockets. Neither woman had ever seen the glasses before and, considerably puzzled by their sudden appearance, they placed them on the stereo set and left the house. When the two returned, they went to look at the glasses again to see if there were any identifying marks on them, but the glasses had disappeared.

This is the kind of dream that is difficult to explain fully. There are elements of astral projection but also elements of dematerialization here, a phenomenon which certainly exists and is well within physical law as we are beginning to understand it today in this age of atomic fusion and fission.

Many astral projections occur during operations or when a person has been anesthetized. These artificial forms of dissociation seem to encourage astral flight, and the records of psychical research are filled with people describing their own operations while hovering above the operating table in a corner of the ceiling.

Mrs. Patricia H. of Ohio was delivering her third baby when she began to hemorrhage and her inner self left her body through her head. She witnessed all that was occurring in the delivery room, as she was suspended above it. She then left the room and visited "with other souls," as she put it, where she was given the choice of staying or returning to the earth plane. Having made her decision to return to earth, she awoke on the operating table, but remembered what she had seen during the period she was apparently unconscious.

Mrs. Arlene W. of Chicago, Illinois has had many psychic experiences over the years. One in particular occurred when her stepson John was having surgery on his arm to repair a severed nerve and tendons. It was a delicate operation and Mrs. W. was justly concerned. During the night of November 11, 1969, when John was already in the hospital, Mrs. W. dreamt that she found herself in his hospital room. She saw him in bed and realized he was in pain, and pushing the call button for a nurse. Mrs. W. was standing behind his bed, looking down. She could see his bandaged arm lying on a pillow on top of the sheets. A nurse came in with a hypodermic needle on a metal tray. Mrs. W. could see her very clearly, the type of cap, color hair, height and build. She watched as the nurse cleaned John's biceps area and injected him with the needle. Almost immediately she could feel him relax. Then, suddenly, Mrs. W. snapped awake, instantly alert. She had an impulse to grab the clock and check the time; it was 2:05 A.M. The following day she went to see her stepson and casually asked him how he had slept. He informed

her that he had had to have a shot at about two in
the morning. Mrs. W. described the nurse she had
"seen" and the description fit the nurse who had
given her stepson the injection. There was no way
in which Mrs. W. could have known this, since this
particular nurse had come on duty at 11 P.M.

Geri Howard of North Hollywood, California
is in her early forties, mother of two girls, aged
eighteen and twenty-two, and lives with an
understanding husband who is aware of her
psychic experiences. The extraordinary astral
projection dream which she reported to me
recently occurred to her on July 6, 1965, which
happened also to be her birthday. At the time her
father, to whom she was very close, was in the
intensive care section of the University of
Minnesota Hospital. A brain tumor had been
removed, and his condition was serious. The night
after her father had had this serious operation,
Mrs. Howard was lying in bed at her aunt's house,
where she, her mother and other relatives were
staying at the time, in order to be close to her
father. Mrs. Howard was listening to her mother
talk, and wondering what would happen if her
father passed away. While her mother was
talking, Mrs. Howard began feeling completely
exhausted. What transpired next is perhaps best
recorded in her own words, since it is a form of
astral projection which differs in some aspects
from the "run-of-the-mill" out-of-the-body experi-

ences, and also because her description of the onset of the state is rather remarkable.

"All of a sudden I felt a funny sensation in my toes, like a tingle, then it gradually went up to my knees and it began to feel as if someone had put a plug into an electric socket and I was being electrified. The feeling went up very gradually with every part becoming electrified till it reached to my head and my whole body felt like a million circuits were running through it. Then it stopped and I was looking down at myself in bed. I thought how funny I was—out, separated, and yet there was the form on the bed that was completely separated from me. I felt I was floating and thought how funny a soul could be hidden inside a body." (During this initial stage, Mrs. Howard's mother kept on talking, but Mrs. Howard could not hear her.)

"I started floating to my father in the hospital bed and then went into his body. I felt I was inside of him and could feel as he felt. I saw through his eyes, my sister, my mother, and me beside in bed. I felt the strength of his arms squeezing to communicate. Then he spoke, using my body on the bed at my aunt's house, to say through my lips from the lifeless form on the bed that we should be strong and always stay together, the three of us, and that we needed our strength more than ever now. These words were coming from my father through my lips. Then I came out of my father's body and traveled back to my own. I entered through my head and then gradually the same process started as before, with the electricity going through the parts of my body as I was entering. I remember when I was halfway in, up to my waist, my mother was saying, what have I done to you? I tried getting back faster but I could not speak or move until I was completely inside. My body was half alive, I could not sit up. The electricity moved down to my knees and then to my toes. When I was completely in my whole body it was again as if I had a million circuits running through me. When it stopped I sat up and was able to speak. I felt as if I had slept for hours and hours, wonderfully refreshed and relaxed."

Mrs. Howard's mother confirmed that for some time before, her daughter had been speaking to her but her voice had not been her own; it was as if someone else were doing the talking. At that time Mrs. Howard had not told her family about her experience.

For a while, Mrs. Howard's father rallied and it looked as if he could leave the hospital. But unfortunately the rally was temporary, there was need for another operation and he passed away during it. Mrs. Howard is glad she could do what she did, and allow her father to pass on to the higher realms with the assurance the family would indeed stick together.

A curious form of astral projection involves a seeming conflict between one part of consciousness and another, perhaps more rationally oriented part.

Sharon M. of Los Angeles reports a number of unusual dreams over the years. Usually, early in the morning, she awakens momentarily and reluctantly decides that it is time to get up. So she does, and goes through the routine of dressing for work, but somehow she goes back to sleep, and when she awakens again she is still in bed.

The dreams are so vivid that she is startled to find that she never left her bed at all. On at least one occasion in 1969 she awoke to see a figure standing at the foot of her bed with its back toward her: even though she could not see the face, she was sure that the figure was herself, or rather an externalization of herself. Such partial projections occur when the conscious mind exercises influence upon the unconscious, which it usually does not do during the sleep state. Or, one might say, the spirit was willing but the body was not.

Mrs. Robert B. is a Maryland housewife who has had ESP experiences for more than thirty years. Contrary to having the usual problems with a husband concerning them, he encouraged her to contact me. Her eldest son is a volunteer fireman and he sleeps in the firehouse on weekends. One particular Saturday night, Mr. B. and his wife were sitting in the living room, watching a late movie on television. Mr. B. sat in his armchair the entire length of the show and did not leave the room. However, Mrs. B., who is normally a light sleeper, immediately went to sleep on the sofa and slept very hard. In fact, on recollection the following day, her husband stated that she was sleeping so deeply that he did not wish to waken her when the show was over, but left her where she was all night.

Mrs. B. dreamt that she heard the noise of fire sirens and equipment arriving nearby. She then arose from the sofa, left her house and walked with her son, the fireman, across the street to their neighbor's unfenced backyard. From there she saw an accident involving several cars one short block from the corner she lived on. Eventually, Mrs. B. started for home, but on awakening had no recollection of reaching it. All the while she was dreaming this, or rather watching it while out of her physical body, the event actually took place precisely as she was "dreaming it." Despite the fact that the sirens were very loud and there was a great deal of noise germane to the arrival of assorted fire equipment, Mrs. B., according to her husband, did not stir, blink, or make any move whatsoever. He thought this rather unusual. However, since he did not know what the accident was all about, he made no mention of it to his wife at breakfast the next morning. Shortly afterward, however, her son came home from duty and began to tell her about it. It was at this point that she remembered the entire incident and described it to her son before he had a chance to tell her more about it. She was able to describe the cars involved, their respective colors, body shapes and positions after the accident. The only variation between what she had dreamt and what had actually happened was the position of her fireman son; in her dream he accompanied her briefly while she went to the scene of the accident while in reality he was on the scene itself, working and aiding the others.

On August 29, 1968, Mrs. B. lay down in a lounge chair on the back porch after dinner and fell asleep. This was most unusual, since she rarely sleeps in the daylight hours. She slept very hard and dreamt that she was at her grandmother's home. While standing under the fruit trees there she could see the dark smoke of a fire about a half mile distant. Having been raised in the area, it was easy for her to pinpoint the approximate place of the fire. When she woke up, she reported the dream to her fireman son, who checked the following day with an officer of his company. A fire had taken place at the location at the time reported by his mother, yet she would have been unable to see it from where she was sleeping.

Mrs. B. describes the state which puzzles her—astral projection—rather well. In her case, it occurred during the period between wakefulness and sleep, when one still is awake but does not realize it. "Your thoughts are under your control, but you do not want to move your body, almost cannot seem to move it. You are perfectly relaxed and on the edge of slipping into sleep. Suddenly there will be an odd but very clear awareness of moving down a straight path or highway at a terrific rate of speed, accelerating rapidly, going on and on until one becomes frightened at the swiftness of progress and wills oneself to stop. This is not easy to do. Sometimes I slow down and then continue as fast as before several times until I finally stop. Sometimes I appear to be close to the ground, at other times high above it. This happens fairly often, I have never reached the end of my journey because of my fears. Next time I will not be too afraid to wait and see what lies at the end of this road I am traveling," she explained.

Mrs. Esther P. is an organist in the San Francisco area. She has had a number of psychic experiences over the years, but the reason she originally contacted me was to learn more about the mechanics of astral projection. She wanted to know if a return to the physical body occurs smoothly or if there is a jolt in connection with it. The incident which prompted this inquiry happened in the 1960s. It was just before five o'clock in the morning when Mrs. P. awoke, a short time before her alarm was set to go off. All at once she was aware that she was *above* her bed, looking down at her body. Then, the alarm went off, and she was on the bed once more, but as she reached out to turn off the alarm, *her hand went right through the clock!* At almost the same time the jolt occurred, and this time she could shut off the alarm.

Mrs. Janet J. of Bowling Green, Kentucky is in her early thirties, the mother of three children and used to ESP incidents through the years. In 1963 she was brought to Lexington Memorial Hospital, having slammed the car door on her thumb. She found herself in severe pain, but suddenly, while lying on a stretcher waiting for a doctor, she felt no pain at all and realized she was out of her body, nearly at the ceiling and looking calmly down at herself. The moment she realized what had happened, however, she was jerked back into her body and the pain resumed. Similarly, when she was given anesthetics during childbirth, she found herself both on the bed, as the participant, and watching "herself" at a distance from somewhere else in the room. Since she was able to describe in great detail what occurred during the birth, she was able to convince her attending physicians of the reality of her out-of-the-body experiences.

An interesting combination of out-of-the-body experiences with survival dream material occurred to Mrs. Eileen Zakhar, a schoolteacher who lives in Illinois. Her father passed away in March 1960; they had been very close and perhaps she grieved more than she should have. A few weeks after his death her father appeared to her in a dream, and they talked. Suddenly she found herself walking with her father in the yard. They had moved into their new home shortly after his death, and he commented on how he liked the yard and the house. They walked up to the street and there he said, "Good-by." He walked into an open lot and Mrs. Zakhar turned to go home. She woke up in her bed. A few nights later the same thing happened once more. Again she walked with her father, and they had a long talk. However, she could not remember what was said. It happened a third time, and again she and her dead father walked to the open lot at the end of their block, only this time, upon awakening, she remembered what her father had said to her.

"It is very pleasant where I am. I am happy now. I will not see you again. I must take a long trip and will be gone for a long time." He smiled at her and walked alone into the empty lot. Then he began to fade, first at the legs, and then up unto the waist. By now Mrs. Zakhar could see through him, but did not move. He turned and looked back at her, but they did not wave at each other. Then he turned away and faded completely. She stood for a while, staring at the empty lot. The next thing she recalls, she awoke in her bed.

Now, a conventional psychiatrist or analyst would classify this dream as simply a desire to make up for the loss of her father, compensate for her grief, by creating a dream image of her late father in conversation with herself. But I am convinced that this subject did indeed experience what she said she did. The difference between a symbolic dream and a clairvoyant dream is considerable, clarity above all making it one of the latter kind. Undoubtedly, Mrs. Zakhar had an out-of-the-body experience, in which state she was as much of the spirit world as was her father. Consequently, they could meet in the dimension which they shared temporarily. If this had been Mrs. Zakhar's only out-of-the-body experience, one might still question my interpretation. However, there are others, these not involving a dead person, but more along the classical lines of astral projection.

The incident I am about to relate happened in September of 1966. The Zakhars had just adopted a small baby. At that time a friend of Mr. Zakhar's invited him to go camping in Wisconsin for a weekend. Since he was very excited about it, his wife didn't have the heart to ask him to stay home although she would have preferred it. The two men had planned on leaving at three o'clock Saturday morning and Mrs. Zakhar did not look forward to the prospect of being alone in the house with the baby. Saturday morning, Mr. Zakhar got up, dressed quietly and went into the kitchen to fix a light breakfast and coffee for his thermos. Mrs. Zakhar heard him but didn't really wake up. She found herself getting out of bed and joined him in the kitchen. The light in the kitchen seemed unusually yellow to her as she stood in the doorway, watching her husband make coffee and toast. However, he seemed to ignore her! Finally she said, "Patty is so tiny, I wish you wouldn't go." He kept right on going with his breakfast. Then he filled the thermos and snapped off the kitchen light, walked past her and went down the stairs, and put on his coat and hat. Again, Mrs. Zakhar asked her husband not to go since both their children were so tiny. Despite her pleas, he left, and Mrs. Zakhar turned to go down the hall. She remembers the night light looked unusually yellow and her feet barely touched the floor. Then she went back to their room, where she discovered herself in bed, and said to herself, quite surprised,

"Well, no wonder he didn't hear me, I'm still in bed sleeping." Then she slid or floated back "into herself" and slept soundly until little Patty cried at 6 A.M.

Since the unconscious rules us during sleep, it is entirely conceivable that it can order our inner selves to leave the physical shell and perform whatever functions the conscious mind does not wish to take, but which the unconscious wishes to perform. Mrs. Zakhar's inner self wanted her husband to stay, but her logical, conscious self had earlier rejected the notion in order not to deprive her husband of his pleasure. With this tension being present between conscious and unconscious minds, the unconscious was able to separate temporarily from the conscious and to make an attempt at delivering the desired message. Unfortunately, Mr. Zakhar was not aware of it because he was in a different dimension. Had he himself also been psychic, perhaps he would have received the message, either partly or in full.

Out-of-the-body experiences are neither frightening nor dangerous, and occur with consistent frequency among all kinds of people. The late founder of the theosophical movement, Madame Helena Blavatsky, stated that astral flight was dangerous because an unwanted, potentially evil soul might enter the body of the traveler while his own soul was in flight elsewhere. She thought that under those circumstances the traveler might not be able to return to his own body, and that the invader might then take over the body of his victim and use it for its own, presumably evil purposes. While it is not entirely impossible to rule out such a situation, I've never come across one, and am convinced that some sort of security mechanism is in operation during astral projections. It may well be that the silver cord, whether it is seen or not, prevents external invasion, or there may be other factors involved, such as an automatic closing of the psychic entrance centers the moment the astral projection takes place. As I have studied many hundreds of possession cases, I am reasonably sure that possession does not come about in the manner feared by Madame Blavatsky.

SURVIVAL
DREAMS

Survival dreams purport to contain communications from the dimension beyond earth, from so-called dead individuals, often referred to as discarnates. These dreams have nothing to do with the survival of the dreamer but tend to prove, when genuine, the continued existence, or survival, of a dead person. Again, many orthodox psychiatrists will brush off such material as wish fulfillment, guilt compensation or other forms of delusion without objective reality and originating entirely in the mind of the dreamer. Undoubtedly, there are dreams involving dead people originating in the unconscious of the dreamer—some people are capable of manufacturing and interacting with the "presence" of a dead relative or friend in the dream state. But the characteristics of such material are quite different from true survival dreams. In the psychic type of survival dream the communication is clear and concise, the discarnate clearly recognizable, and usually, though not always, there is a message attached which becomes objective reality only *after* the dream, or which may have meaning only to a specific individual, not necessarily the dreamer him/herself. There are cases containing other telltale marks, such as a dead person wearing certain clothes or accessories which he/she actually wore at the time of death, without the dreamer, however, being aware of this fact. Or there may be references to third parties which are meaningless to the dreamer, but which are checked afterward and found to be relevant and correct. In other words, the survival dream material I am presenting here is of the type that is very hard to dismiss as imaginary, unless, of course, one sets out to do this at all costs, even at the cost of distorting the truth.

Roughly half of all the communications from the so-called beyond occur in the dream state, because it appears to be easier for discarnates to reach people in the physical dimension while they are asleep. I have already explained that the loosening of bonds between the conscious and the unconscious in the sleep state allows for an easier entry of such material. Since psychic perception is realized not with the physical senses but with an underlying finer, inner set of sensory organs, the exclusion of the external perception organs during the sleep state is of course advantageous. In this manner the communicator need not work through the denser layer of the physical sensory organs but can make direct contact with the inner set of perception organs, that have been laid bare, so to speak, in the dream state. It is a little like cooking potatoes after removing their skin: if the skin is first removed, the potatoes will cook faster and will be pliable sooner, if they are cooked in the skin, the heat will have to penetrate the skin first and more time and energy will be necessary to accomplish the cooking. The temporary setting aside of the external body, just like the skin of the potato, enables the communicator to reach the inner body quicker and with greater clarity.

Above all it should be remembered that this category of psychic dreams is strongly motivated—survival dreams have a purpose. They contain a message which may differ in impact and importance from case to case, but is nevertheless always present. The dead do not contact the living idly, except perhaps to prove their continued existence in another dimension. But one can scarcely call this an idle cause since the proof of survival of a loved one constitutes a major factor in the lives of many people, especially those who have by their upbringing or environmental pressures been unable to grasp this kind of truth before. There is always a reason why dead individuals, or spirits, if you prefer that term, get in touch with flesh and blood people during dream states. If the reason is not altogether clear upon awakening, it may become so eventually. But it is best for the dreamer to assume there is a definite, specific purpose for the survival dream to occur, and not to dismiss it simply as "one of those things."

Not all survival dreams are as dramatic as the one reported by the Washington *Daily News* of

May 7, 1969. According to the newspaper, a mother in Karachi, Pakistan dreamt on May 7 that an old man in white told her to dig up the grave of her two-year-old daughter, fifty hours after the funeral. When she told the story to her neighbors, she was laughed at. But a few believed her and went to the cemetery to open the grave. The child was still alive and sucking her thumb when the coffin was opened. The mother's psychic dream had saved its life. Who the spirit communicator was, has not been reported. Evidently someone "on the Other Side" felt that the time for the child had not yet arrived, and decided to intervene.

Louise S. lives in Ohio. She is a housewife in her late thirties, who has been married for twenty-two years, and has three children. She is interested in ESP, mainly because of her own experiences in this field. On August 8, 1968, she dreamt that her father-in-law, who had passed away five months before, knocked on her door. He told her that the holidays were very sad for him and kept shaking his head. He then warned Mrs. S. of the holiday season ahead. On awakening Mrs. S. clearly remembered the dream and looked toward the holidays with some apprehension. In December of the same year she became very ill with the flu, and on December 27 she received word that her mother-in-law had passed away. But these two events were not the only reasons for her holiday season being sad, because the death brought additional heartache through an estate dispute following the mother-in-law's demise.

Mrs. Judy Hendrick is in her early thirties, mother of three children and married to an Illinois police officer who does not share her interest in ESP. Ever since she was eight years old, Mrs. Hendrick has had premonitory and other ESP experiences which have led her to believe that she has a considerable talent in this respect. In July 1961, she had a dream in which her late father appeared to her along with one of her favorite uncles, Joe K. This convinced Mrs. Hendrick that her uncle had also passed over. The following morning she told her husband, but he advised her not to worry about it. Nevertheless, her fears persisted, so she wrote to her mother, inquiring whether her Uncle Joe was well. It was then that her mother explained that her Uncle Joe had indeed died of leukemia, but as Mrs. Hendrick had been expecting a baby at the time the family had decided not to tell her until after the baby had been born. There was no way in which Mrs. Hendrick could have known of her uncle's fatal illness, firstly, because it wasn't discovered until very near his death, and secondly, because he lived over 2,000 miles away from her.

In August 1968 Mrs. Hendrick went to work as a cocktail waitress at a club where her coworkers were the two daughters of the owner. They became friends, and when one of the girls, Janet, was to be married shortly, Mrs. Hendrick was invited to the wedding. That night her father appeared to her in a dream and warned her that the wedding would be postponed because of an auto accident involving Janet's fiance. Shortly after, she awoke, when her husband, who was serving in the police force, came home and informed her that there had been a bad accident involving a truck and a car. Unfortunately, he did not remember the names of the persons involved. While he was speaking, Mrs. Hendrick felt she should call Janet to see whether her fiance was all right, but early the next morning before she could call there was a telephone call from Janet's sister, informing Mrs. Hendrick that the wedding was being postponed because of an auto accident in which Janet's fiance had been involved.

The fascinating thing about this type of dream is the apparent ability by some discarnates at certain times to let their kin or friends on the earth plane in on some advance information, as a cushion against upsets or impending tragedy. Even these partial glimpses into the future reinforce my conviction that events are predetermined by some sort of law, and that those who have gone on into the next dimension are frequently able to "read" events ahead of *our* time, sometimes allowing us to share their advance information. In many cases the elements causing an event to happen are not even brought together at the time when a prophetic dream of this kind is received, yet the information is already complete!

Edwin M. is a real estate broker in his late sixties who lives in California. Some of his dream prophecies come true the following day, others as much as ten years later. During World War II Mr. M. had a dream in which his mother appeared to him, saying, "Your cousin Harry is dead." Two days later Mr. M. received a letter from his mother, stating that a telegram had been received from the War Department, informing her the cousin was missing in action.

Now, the interesting thing about this dream is that Mr. M.'s mother was living at the time of the dream. Why didn't Cousin Harry himself appear to the dreamer to tell him that he had passed over? The answer is fairly simple: Harry was able to make contact with Mr. M.'s mother, but not with Mr. M. directly, for the same reason that some psychics cannot reach certain people while they are excellent with others. But apparently the contact did not result in Mr. M.'s mother getting the message of Harry's passing, while Mr. M. did. Only by including Mr. M.'s mother in his projected message was Cousin Harry able to let his family know of his passing.

Not only are some of these extraterrestrial sources, spirit guides, if you wish, extremely articulate, but they have the ability to pinpoint events rather precisely, which is something most mediums on the earth cannot do very well.

Mrs. Margaret R., whom I have mentioned earlier in this book, was engaged to an Air Force officer during World War II. She and her fiance had been separated for two and a half years, so it was only natural that she should be very unhappy when they were separated again shortly after their formal engagement. Every night after he left she prayed for him and often awoke in tears. One night, in 1944, when he had been gone about a week, she had a strange dream in which she saw herself standing in the kitchen, reading a letter from him as the tears streamed down her face. Suddenly she heard a woman's voice speaking to her, saying, "Do not cry, Margaret, he will be home October 26." Then the voice ceased and Mrs. R. woke up.

What was strange about the dream was the fact that the voice, which she did not recognize, had called her Margaret while her nickname Meg was usually used by everyone else. The dream occurred in the last week of May, and as the weeks and months went by, she found herself waiting expectantly, certain that the dream would come true, even though her fiance was in the South Pacific. She told her family and friends of her dream. Then on October 24 she received a telegram from her fiance, advising her that he was in Miami and would be home in a few days. Sure enough, on October 26 at 10:30 P.M., the doorbell rang, and there he was.

Evidently the information obtained from these sources is more reliable than human evaluation or likelihood. Many years later Mrs. R.

dreamt that her sister, who makes her home in California, would come home for a visit, coming alone and by airplane. When she discussed this with her mother, her mother assured her that her sister was not expected, and if she came, would certainly not come without her husband and son. A few days later, nevertheless, the sister did arrive. She was alone, and came by air.

Mrs. Virginia Fleming describes herself as "an average housewife," mother of five children, no profession, who makes her home in Massachusetts. One night in 1962 she had gone to bed early but woke up with a shock because of a voice she heard in a dream. It was a voice filled with apprehension and urgency, which she did not recognize although she thought at first that it was her father calling her. All the voice said was, "Jini." Mrs. Fleming looked at her watch and found it was 12:03 A.M. Without thinking, she left her bed and went downstairs to call the police, though she did not know why. Nevertheless she felt that she had to call. As she picked up the telephone, a man's voice came on although the phone had not rung. It turned out to be the local police department informing her that her husband had been in an accident. The car was a total wreck although her husband had only been shaken up.

Six years later, on November 22, 1968, she had another experience of a similar kind. Again she had gone to bed rather early, and was awakened by the same voice calling to her, just her name, "Jini." Again, she looked at her watch, and found it was 11:33 P.M. At the same time she remembered having heard in a dream the sound of a body falling hard on pavement. It was so real, in fact, that she got up and walked down to the street to see whether it had actually happened in front of her house. Immediately she assumed that something had happened to her husband, but she didn't know until the following morning what the voice had warned her about. At 7:00 A.M. she heard on the news that her first cousin, Lawrence, had been killed by a car while crossing the street. The accident happened at precisely 11:33 P.M., the moment when the voice had entered her dream.

Mrs. M. S. lives in the Middle West, and is active in the educational field. She has a long list of psychic experiences from early childhood onward. But the dream which I have found particularly interesting in relation to this chapter occurred in early 1975.

"My father appeared to me in a dream and asked me to look in a certain dresser drawer, which we had recently brought from another state to our home and I had not yet taken time to go through. When I awoke and looked, there were some traveler's checks from 1963 which I was unaware of. Since our budget had been rather taxed that month, I was very glad to get them. I had not consciously thought of my father for several days, and even if he were in my subconscious, I certainly was not thinking of the traveler's checks—in fact, I was not even aware of their presence."

Mrs. Susannah D. of New Jersey, already mentioned earlier in this book, reports an interesting survival dream. In high school she had become acquainted with a young man named Tony. She dated him occasionally, but no serious relationship ensued. Later on they went their separate ways and she hadn't seen him or heard of him or his family for about eight or ten years. Also, Mrs. D. had since married and had a two-year-old daughter at the time the dream occurred, in August of 1948. In the dream, Tony came to her, and it appeared that he was in an airplane cracking up on the ground. He was screaming her name, "Sue, help me," over and over. Mrs. D. awoke in a sweat, and after talking it over with her husband, decided to try and reach Tony's family. When she did, she was informed that the family had received a telegram on the very date of her dream, but *one year* before stating that Tony had been killed in a plane crack-up during the invasion of Normandy.

Why Mrs. D. received this message after the event and not simultaneously with the event, is perhaps not as hard to explain as it might seem at first glance. Possibly the message *was* "sent out" at the time of the tragedy but failed to reach her. On the anniversary, the discarnate, Tony, remembering his tragedy and going over it again, his thoughts might then have reached out to his former friend. Anniversaries of emotional events frequently carry greater weight than any other time after the event itself.

Rose T. of Vienna, Austria, reports an interesting dream under the postmark of October 24, 1974. She was living with her aged mother, and a brother who had turned into an alcoholic and was considered a threat to the rest of the family. Because of the excitement, Mrs. T.'s mother passed away on October 27, 1973. Shortly before she died, she confided to her daughter Rose, "Should I not return from the hospital then I will come for my son, because he is no good." Due to an accident, the alcoholic son also died, on January 27, 1974. The night before the funeral, Rose had a dream in which she walked from her room into a smaller room where she saw her mother seated on the bed, as if she were still alive. The mother said, "Rose, I am going to come with you today." To which the daughter, in the dream, replied, "Mother, that is impossible, you are no longer alive." But the mother insisted that she would come along with her daughter. The following day, at the funeral for her brother, Rose was completely alone, since there were no other relatives, or close friends. Under the circumstances her mother's company, although unseen, was a real relief.

Mrs. Regina Rudinger of New York City reports a most unusual dream, which occurred to her sister, Mrs. M. S. of Boston. In the dream a brother, who had passed away previously, made contact with Mrs. S., demanding that his body be disinterred from the cemetery and moved to a different part because of deep water accumulating in his grave. The family hesitated to do anything about this, and discussed it with religious authorities. Finally, they received authorization from the board of health and the grave was opened. It turned out that the discarnate brother's complaint was based on fact: the grave was filled with water, and the body was therefore moved to a drier site. The original grave is still empty.

In a second dream, the same brother requested that his mother be stopped from visiting his grave. This sounded strange to the surviving daughters, until they discovered that their mother had been making the exhausting trip to the grave day in, day out, although she was in poor health at the time and such a trip represented a great strain.

That the dead are very much concerned with the affairs of the living is not exactly news. However, many dead take their earth life concepts with them into the next dimension.

Mrs. Anna S. of Pittsburgh, Pennsylvania originally lived in New York for forty years. She had a cousin by the name of Albert, who was ailing, and who was taken to Bellevue Hospital for treatment. She wanted to visit him, but being ill herself, she kept postponing it time and again.

Another cousin named Rudolph kept her informed of Albert's condition, however. Early one morning around five o'clock, Mrs. S. woke from a heavy sleep. She had dreamt that her cousin Albert had come to see her and that she was glad to see him. "I've come to say good-by," he said to her in the dream. "I am going home and will go into business with my brother Ignatz." Even in her dream it sounded funny to Mrs. S., because she realized that Ignatz had been dead for years. In the morning, the telephone rang. It was Rudolph informing her that Albert had passed away that morning at 5 A.M.

The desire to communicate with relatives or friends at the moment of death is both understandable and common.

Mrs. Margaret M. of Pennsylvania was taking a nap on Sunday, December 7, 1941, when she was awakened by her brother's voice calling her "Sis." Still partially in her dream, she saw his head and army cap, moving from the far corner of the ceiling downward. When she collected herself she noticed her pillow was wet with tears. She knew that her brother was a corporal in the Army but she had no idea where he was stationed. A little later she learned that the United States had been attacked by Japan, and her brother, who had been stationed on Oahu, Hawaii, was one of those killed in the first day of war.

Some survival dreams deliver a message more in the philosophical vein, perhaps to acquaint surviving relatives or friends with the discarnates' continued existence in another dimension, of their happy state, or perhaps to inform them concerning that other world through which we all pass at one time.

I have already mentioned Mrs. Helen J., who lives in upstate New York and one of whose sons passed away tragically. In June 1966, she had a dream in which she became aware of being in a higher spiritual world, out of the earth of mortal man, as she put it. She saw herself standing in a very beautiful room, aware of beautiful colors and a sense of happiness beyond human feeling and description. "Suddenly I knew that God was granting me the blessing of being able to speak to my son this night," Mrs. J. relates. "He appeared before me and embraced me. We spoke through thought transference. I said, 'Tell me, David, what is it like over there?' My son replied, 'Mother, it is beautiful over here and no one grows old. Earth is the pathway to hell.' I then asked him if I could go with him and he put his arm out as if to stop me and said, 'No, not yet, but you will be here before the end of the world.'"

Mrs. Rosemarie C., a housewife living in Ohio, has had a number of psychic dreams. Some years ago she and her husband were living at the home of her mother. Next door lived an elderly man by the name of K. Mrs. C. did not know the neighbor personally but in passing they sometimes nodded to each other. One night she had a strange dream. She saw a shadowy figure of a man behind a frosted glass shower door. The figure did not appear to have clothes on, and the man was waving his arms frantically and calling out the name of a girl, which, however, she could not make out in the dream. Then the figure became motionless and slumped against the glass door, sliding down to the floor. When she woke up the following morning, there were police cars and an ambulance at her neighbor's house. Mr. K. had been found dead of a heart attack, his telephone off the hook. Evidently he had tried to call his daughter but had been unable to get through. Somehow he had manage to pierce the consciousness of his psychic neighbor, however, and at the very moment of his death made contact with her.

"Should I disregard this dream or attempt to do something about it?" asks Jillianne A. of Pennsylvania concerning a most unusual dream which has recurred to her several times. Her dream is about Brian Epstein, the late English manager of the Beatles. He appeared in her dreams looking very haggard and tired, and in despair. She described him as having a cut under his left eye and having lost a great deal of weight. He comes to her and she takes him to places she has never been to before, yet she seems to know all about them and she brings him up to date on what has happened with the Beatles since he died. In each dream, the ex-manager asks her to warn the Beatles and insists that she must contact them. Miss A. has never met Brian Epstein nor does she know the Beatles personally. But she does confess to being an avid fan of the group and considers herself a "walking Beatle encyclopedia." She is twenty-five years old. Under the circumstances one might easily assume that her emotional interest in the group could have conjured up the figure of the ex-manager in the dreams. On the other hand, it might also be the other way around; *because* of her emotional involvement with the Beatles, and because she is psychic, could the ex-manager in his dimension not have sought her out to carry his message to the group?

Finally, a dream of my own, which seems to fit into this category also. My father passed away July 25, 1966, while I was in Ireland. I was about to go abroad again in the summer of 1968, when I wondered how my father was getting on in the next dimension. The night of July 4, I had a vivid dream in which I saw my father on the telephone, speaking to me in a very loud voice. "I'm all right. I'm all right," he said, repeating the phrase several times, as if to reassure me. That was all there was to this dream but it was strong and almost as if in answer to my musings of the night before. Dreams of this kind are not proof in the conventional sense of the term, but they may very well fit into the category of survival dreams along with many more detailed and evidential ones.

REINCARNATION DREAMS

This is the stuff that some commercial novels are made of: recurrent dreams of previous lives, usually very colorful, which keep on recurring and puzzling the dreamer. Unfortunately, not all reincarnation dreams are as precise or as insistent. The majority of this type of dream is partial, fragmentary, hazy and altogether frustrating in that it leaves the dreamer with the feeling of having been given some sort of unusual glance at his or her own past without spelling it out so one could go to the nearest library and look it all up.

Reincarnation dreams are dreams in which the individual sees him or herself going through actions or in places with which he or she is not familiar in conscious existence. They differ from the first two categories of dreams in precisely the same areas in which all psychic dreams differ from "ordinary" dreams, by being specific and, even when fragmentary, sharp and fully remembered upon awakening. In particular, reincarnation dreams have a habit of coming in series, usually exact repetitions of one dream, more rarely partial repetition with follow-ups. An often asked question with this type of dream is whether it may be due to clairvoyance—a discarnate's attempt to communicate to the dreamer his or her story. This argument is easily dismissed: those who have reincarnation dreams are rarely, if ever, psychic before or after the occurrence of such dreams and have shown no particular talents with ESP in other areas. Also, true reincarnation dreams leave a residue of restlessness, a compulsion to do something about the dream that is not present with other types of dreams. In the dream, the dreamer sees himself looking different from his present appearance and yet he knows that it is himself and it is to him all these things are happening. With other types of psychic dreams, a scene is seen but the dreamer himself is the observer, not the participant, except of course with dreams pertaining to the future, in which an event that has not yet come to pass is being shown to the dreamer. In that case he may appear in the dream as his present self, looking exactly as he does when he goes to bed. But reincarnation dreams always deal with the past, therefore the dreamer never looks the way he does in his present life.

Conventional psychiatrists may dismiss such dreams as fantasies, wish-fulfillment dreams, meaningless romanticizing of present-day events, and altogether connected with the personality of the dreamer without containing so much as an ounce of information from the dreamer's earlier lives. They do not accept reincarnation as a valid theory. But it is difficult to explain by such criteria the number of verified reincarnation dreams on record. When the dreamer remembers upon awakening a dream in which he saw himself as a different person in a different age, when he remembers names, data and circumstances from the past with which he is not familiar in his present life, and to which he has no access, if he wanted to research it, and when such material is subsequently proven to be authentic, and the personality referred to by the dreamer actually existed, then it is very difficult indeed to blame it all on the personality quirks of the *present* person.

Reincarnation memories come to some people at various times in their lives, but the majority of us never have them. It is my conviction from the studies I have undertaken, that only where a previous lifetime has in some way been cut short or has been tragic, is the individual given part of the memory as a sort of bonus to influence his or her present conduct. The lives of people who have had full lives prior to the present one are never remembered, neither in dreams nor in so-called waking flashes or in *deja vu*, which is a phenomenon sometimes related to reincarnation memories. Most *deja vu* is simply precognitive experiences which are not realized at the time they occur but are remembered when the precognitive experience becomes objective reality. Some *deja vu*, especially that which is more involved and contains precise and detailed information about places and situations the perceiver is not familiar with, is due to reincarnation memories. All *deja vu* occurs in the waking state and is therefore not properly within the scope of this work, but it is related to reincarnation dreams, in that it also discloses to the individual some hidden material from his or her own past.

With the flood of interesting dreams occurring to people all over the world, we must guard against overenthusiasm when it comes to potential reincarnation material. To begin with, only recurrent dreams need be considered here. That is, dreams that occur to the dreamer a number of times in repetitive fashion, and that contain more or less the same material. I have found that reincarnation material forces itself on the unconscious mind of the sleeper, perhaps because it wants to be acknowledged so that the lessons of a previous lifetime may be applied to the present. Together with waking flashes of prior life memories, recurrent dreams form the bulk of material where hypnosis may be of practical use. Through a method called hypnotic regression, the individual is taken back first to his or her own childhood and then gradually to the threshold of birth, and beyond it into a presumed earlier lifetime. This is done in stages and success depends upon the ability of the subject to go into the hypnotic state. If successful, it will result in loosening the memory and allow the subject to relate his or her earlier experiences freely and to describe the scenes from previous lives in greater detail than was possible in the recurrent dreams. Also, the hypnotherapist can excise unpleasant memories from previous lifetimes at the same time, while bringing to the surface details of such lives which may be checked out in conventional records.

I have undertaken this type of regression many times with suitable subjects, but never with anyone who simply wanted to be regressed in order to find out who he or she might have been in a previous life. Not only do I feel that such attempts are bound to fail and would not produce any information, but I find such attempts morally objectionable because it seems to me that reincarnation memories occur to people to whom they *ought to* occur and not to others. In artificially ferreting out such hidden material, might we not hurt the individual's karmic progress? In a previous book, entitled *Born Again*, I reported some of the extraordinary dreams of a number of subjects that proved to be authentic material from past lives. Since then, new cases have come to my attention, proving that reincarnation dreams are not altogether rare.

Where then does one draw the line between fantasy dreams and material capable of verification? As with all dreams, we must take into account the individual's background, education, ability to involve him or herself with the subject of his or her dreams, and other personal factors which differ from individual to individual. Let us assume that someone dreams of a life in ancient Egypt, but has a working knowledge of Egyptology, or perhaps a personal interest in the field. Then we must look at such dreams with the jaundiced eye of the doubter: was the dream material suggested by conscious knowledge of the dreamer, flushed out as cleverly as the unconscious is able to, or are we dealing here with reincarnation? Are memories of life in ancient Egypt *causing* the dreamer to pursue a study of that period in his or her current life?

It is important to determine what came first, the dream or the interest in the subject matter. Anyone judging the veridicality of reincarnation dreams without personally being familiar with the subject or at the very least with a full transcript of the dreams and the background of the dreamer, will not arrive at any fair conclusion concerning the authenticity of such material. Opinions are not facts.

Karen G. is in her middle twenties, a member of the United States Air Force, stationed abroad. She has had three recurrent dreams which have remained with her vividly and disturbingly. Her husband, unfortunately, puts no stock in such material, so Mrs. G. contacted me to put it on record. When she was twenty-one she dreamt of a woman in a long, dark dress and a white apron—a good-looking woman with long black hair and green eyes. People full of hatred were shouting at her and tying her to a tree. They put brush under her feet and kept yelling, "Burn her, burn the witch!" She cried that she was not a witch and that if she were they would never have had a chance to burn her. "When she said that, I suddenly realized with quite a shock that I was this girl. I was watching this in full color and I somehow knew that I was her," Mrs. G. explained.

The woman in Mrs. G.'s dream tried to make people understand that she "just knew things," and that was all. When they wouldn't listen, she called them fools. Then the people lit the fire. It was horrible to the dreamer because she knew that she was innocent, she knew she was trying to get through to them. "I felt the heat of the fire and knew her anguish one last time, that they were wrong and someday they would know it."

Mrs. G. did not get any details, although for some reason the names Elizabeth and Suzanne come to her mind in connection with this dream. She has never been able to forget it and it has troubled her a great deal; she has dreamt it at least three times.

The second dream was about another woman, who was dressed in a long dress. Somehow Mrs. G. knew this was in France. The woman was at a party in a large mansion and the dreamer knew that she was either the wife or mistress of the man who owned the mansion. In the dream she saw a game being played, where one person was sent from the room while the others hid. When the person came back he was blind-folded. In this scene it was the owner of the mansion and he had to look for the woman. While he was feeling his way around the room looking for her, the others moved the furniture around to confuse him. He thought it was fun at first, but then he began to get angry and the woman got scared. "That is when I knew I was her. I ran and hid in a closet. Then the dream switched to a little town and the woman was arguing with a man and he said if she continued to keep doing something he would take their baby away from her. She then got hysterical and threatened to commit suicide. Then the dream switched back to the mansion again, showing her crying and pleading with this man. She then opened the French doors, ran out on the balcony and jumped off." That was the end of the dream.

Mrs. G. dreamt it when she was twenty-one and again about a year later, at which time she suddenly felt inside that the man of this dream was now the man she worked for.

(It is not unusual for people with reincarnation dreams to feel that certain individuals now living may be reincarnated from the same period as the dream. Usually, people the dreamer has known in a past life are now in a different position and usually quite unaware of the connection. It is of course difficult to prove this unless they also have recurrent dreams or some form of recognition that a previous lifetime has connected them with that person.)

The third dream which so disturbed Mrs. G. was rather short. She saw a woman and a child, and it seems that a volcano had erupted and the lava was coming down all around them. All the woman could think of was to save the child; she grabbed it and ran as fast as she could up a path and finally made it to a place which looked like a city or village built into a mountain; the windows were protected by sliding glass. "I remember a feeling of relief when they went inside and stood watching the lava come down. In the last part of the dream the whole place began to rumble and shake."

Now, the interesting thing about these three dreams is that they have one thing in common (that is, if the third dream also leads to sudden death). In the first dream, Mrs. G. is a witch burned at the stake, in the second she jumps to her death, and in the third she is a victim of a natural catastrophe—all three lives cut short by *external forces*.

Mrs. Shirley F. of Denver, Colorado, has had a number of recurrent dreams over the past twenty-five years. She sees a large castle, always the same one, but a different room each time. She cannot make out the location of this castle but knows that it is situated on a cliff in rugged terrain and overlooks an ocean. In the dreams, she is always strolling through it leisurely, at times looking for someone, but always with the feeling of being at home.

On the surface of it, one might say that dreaming of a castle, especially if one is in modest circumstances, is simply another form of romantic wish fulfillment. But this need not be so: a large percentage of the European population lived in some form of mansion or castle, not necessarily as the owner, and if this recurrent dream refers to the Middle Ages or a period prior to, let us say 1800, dreaming of a castle as home is not altogether unusual. Unfortunately, with so little to go on, there is no way in which an identity in a previous lifetime can be proven.

Chris Roberts, thirty years old, was working toward his bachelor's degree in social case work, when he first contacted me in 1970. The young man has had a number of experiences which lead him to believe that he has lived before, perhaps several times. One particular dream incident stands out. When he was working at a private, non-profit rehabilitation center in upstate New York, he met a young woman named Josephine F. Instantly on meeting, they recognized each other as if they had known each other before, which in fact they had not. As time went on they have come to realize a mutual former existence, perhaps as husband and wife, in Japan at some previous time. Even though Miss F. is Italian, she looks to Mr. Roberts astonishingly oriental, and his daily living habits are also somewhat oriental.

One night, while many miles apart, both individuals dreamt the identical dream at the same time, and related it to each other the following day, Miss F. starting at the beginning, and Mr. Roberts coming in at the middle and telling it to the end, much to their mutual amazement. They dreamt of some natural catastrophe in earlier times, during which they were both thrown into the sea. They remember swimming in a tumultuous sea, surrounded by other struggling survivors until they were somehow able to crawl inside a floating house. From a window in the house, they were able to watch the approaching onslaught of a great wave that finally engulfed and drowned them both.

Not all reincarnation dreams are clearly defined, with a beginning, middle, and end; sometimes the end is left in doubt. Also, occasionally symbolic dream material pertaining to the present lifetime becomes intermingled with reincarnation dreams and confuses the issue. Such material is particularly hard to interpret.

Claudia L. lives in Michigan, is in her late twenties and had a recurrent dream from the time she was five years old until she turned thirteen. In this dream she was always a child of about five years. She and her mother had gone into a tall building which she compared to a skyscraper. Her mother, and another adult who appeared in the dream, had left her alone while they went to a business appointment in the building and somehow the little girl got separated from them. She did not miss her companions but wandered around the great, vaulted reception area, noticing colored shop windows, flowers and a variety of people. Among the decorations there were some tall jars, large enough for her to jump into. As she wandered about she realized that the building was deserted, as if she had gotten trapped inside it after working hours, and then she heard someone approaching down a hallway. She thought it was a night watchman coming to see what she was doing. But the man appeared to be wearing a coat of mail. He came after the little girl in a menacing way, and she started to run. She was afraid, in the dream, that she was going to be stabbed to death with the man's lance, but then she managed to lose him by jumping into one of the large jars. He went clanking by, and at this point there was a blotting out of the dream.

Miss L. does not know whether the pot was smashed and she was found, or whether she had managed to fool her pursuer. On awakening, however, she always felt that she had left something unfinished or left someone behind. Because of the seeming absurdity of a mail-clad night watchman pursuing her in what appeared to be a modern building, Miss L. dared not mention the dream to anyone lest she be ridiculed. But why was the dream recurring to her, and why was she unsettled by its content? Could it not be that the tall building or perhaps the watchman's coat of mail was an interposition from another type dream?

Dreams shared by more than one person are much rarer than single dreams.

Richard U. of New York State in 1970 dreamt of a very strange scene. In the dream he was astride a horse on a beach, waiting for a ship. There was a group of men with him, dressed in what he later realized was armor like that worn by the crusaders. The water seemed very blue and crystal clear.

The following day he mentioned this dream to two close friends. It then developed that both had dreamt of being on an old ship. They were dressed in flowing robes, heading for an island, and they, too, had been impressed with the crystal clear blue water. Had the three of them seen the same scene from a different point of view, because they had been in it together in a previous lifetime?

Mrs. Georgia G. has always felt that she once lived in the Old West, that is, in another lifetime. Right now, she lives in Iowa, is in her early thirties, married for the second time, and the mother of two children. Her background is English and German, as it is with many of the people in her part of the Middle West.

The first dream which made her wonder about having lived before happened to her rather unexpectedly. The scene showed a beautiful summer day, and it was either noon or very early afternoon since the sun was shining overhead. She saw a town square with one side bordered by a huge, long stone wall; the center of the town square seemed shaded. There were two padres standing there looking down on a young woman who was kneeling before them. Georgia could not see their faces since they were in the shaded area, but the woman seemed to be around thirty years old and had on drab, dark clothes. There was a crowd of people at the end of the wall in the distance, cowering away from the middle of the square where these three figures were. The woman, speaking in English, said, "I beg of you, have mercy on me." She was pleading with the two priests but they only watched her in stony silence. All at once she knew she was that woman! She looked at the crowd in the distance but could see they didn't want to get mixed up in the affair, whatever it was.

Although the dream occurred to her only once, it was of such clarity and power that she could not forget it afterward. Also, she remembered that when she was a child, her parents had the greatest difficulty getting her to go to Sunday school. She would pretend that she was sick in order to get out of having to go, and even now she does not go to church. Had she been made to suffer in a previous lifetime because of psychic ability? From her description, the two padres may have been eighteenth—or early nineteenth-century priests, in what was then the Spanish part of North America. Unfortunately, her dream cannot be pinpointed any further, but to her it is like a corridor to another lifetime.

There are many cases on record of dreams relating to previous incarnations, but dreams relating to the "transitional period," or the very moment of "coming back" are very rare indeed. Perhaps this is so because according to karmic law that is one part of the experience one is not supposed to remember. At any rate, I have reported some of these instances in *Born Again*, where the process of forgetting one lifetime and being made ready for another is described. There is mention of a "well of forgetfulness," the water of which accomplishes this remarkable feat.

Mrs. P. L. is a divorced woman in her early fifties who lives in the South. Her studies included three years of pre-med, and at one time she taught at a secretarial school. Mrs. L. dreams in color, and in French and Hebrew, languages she neither speaks nor understands. But the dream that interested me most occurred to her in 1938.

She dreamt that she went into a circular enclosure with a fountain in the center. There were small cubicles covered with curtains and she was told to go into one of them to "receive." Inside was a water pipe which she smoked until she lost consciousness. When she awoke the following morning, she was in a stupor for over an hour, something very unusual for her. Had she had a glimpse at the "machine" used by the powers that be to make people forget their previous life experiences, in order to be properly prepared for the next one?

There are many valid techniques of reinforcing one's ability to remember dreams upon awakening, if that is necessary. I find that on the whole true psychic dreams do not require much reinforcing because they are rarely forgotten, certainly not quickly. Nevertheless, there may be people who for one or another reason are unable to recall more than a fragment of unusual dreams.

Just as waking flashes of previous lives may be triggered by actually passing through a place where one has lived before, or by meeting someone whom one instinctively feels one has known before, so dreams of this type can be triggered by external, realistic experiences prior to sleep.

For instance, someone may pass through a strange town, which he does not know consciously. At night, he has a reincarnation dream in which he finds himself in the same place, but in an earlier age. In such a case the dream was triggered by his actual passing through the town, although he did not receive any impression of previous experiences while awake.

These experiences differ from person to person and have a lot to do with the individual and his or her makeup. In some, reincarnation material finds it easier to get to the surface than in others, and it is entirely conceivable that material of this nature can lie dormant for many years until an external event brings it to the surface or triggers its appearance in the dream state. Much of the material of this kind is fragmentary and no more than a flash or a small portion of a previous existence. When there is unfinished business, so to speak, and the person is to receive a detailed message which will help him or her cope better with his present existence, the reincarnation dream is longer and far more detailed than these common sudden flashes or one-time memories.

When I said earlier that recurrent dreams are a sign of reincarnation memories, I did not mean to exclude single dreams of this nature. They, too, can have reincarnation content, but it is my experience with the material with which I am familiar, that in the majority of cases, if not all, additional material comes to the surface sooner or later. Even when dreams are not recurrent or parallel, there may be dreams connected with each other, or dreams dreamt in part at various times in a person's present life. A great deal of reincarnation material manifests itself in hunches or strange attractions to places and people, which are hard to verbalize or even rationalize. Nevertheless, they come from the same source as the more elaborate dreams do. It is my conviction that previous lives imprint themselves upon the psyche of each person, and stay in place when subsequent layers of consciousness are added on top. Thus a so-called "old soul" consists of a substantial number of layers of consciousness. From time to time, the earlier layers of experience protrude or intrude into the present existence, giving information or conveying feelings alien to the person in his or her present circumstances. We are at all times the sum total of our previous lives, even if we fail to remember them in the conscious state.

Lastly, there is a category of reincarnation dream, usually recurrent, which I would like to call *fear dreams*. They have to do with the *manner* in which a person passed on in a previous existence. Because of it, they cast a shadow, so to speak, over the present existence. Sometimes the anxiety ceases abruptly when a certain age is reached, and the dreams stop. In other cases, the dreams represent a problem and may lead to psychological disturbances or maladjustments. In such cases hypnotherapy is indicated. I have hypnotically regressed such people, with the approval of their physicians, when I thought I could excise the fear dream in the process. Of course, all reincarnation memories are due to unfinished lives of one kind or another, but with fear dreams, the manner of death is particularly violent or strongly remembered, more than the rest of the dream, to the point where it may become an obsession with similar circumstances if and when they occur in the present incarnation.

Mrs. Margaret K., age forty, married, mother of three children, native of Mississippi, but currently residing in Kentucky, got in touch with me after she had read *Born Again*. My earlier book gave her the courage to come forward with the startling experiences of her life. "*Born Again* is the most intriguing book I have ever read on reincarnation; never before have I felt such an impulse to write an author," she began.

Mrs. K. has worked at various jobs: secretary, bookkeeper, salesperson, waitress. Beginning when she was a small child of six or seven, she had a recurrent dream until she was well into her teens. In the dream she was on the ground and flames were leaping up from it all around her. But when the flames reached to within a small circle of her, they would come no closer. Next she would find herself in the middle of water. The flames would start from the shoreline and proceed toward her, always stopping before they reached her. She would awaken from these dreams very much disturbed.

Mrs. K. is one of those few who does have ESP, despite her reincarnation dreams. In recent years she had another recurrent dream, about a man connected with the sea. She believes herself to be his wife or sweetheart in the dream, but there is always something keeping them apart. When she awakes from these dreams she feels a deep sense of loss and something like grief. All day long she will remember the man, yet she does not know who he is.

There may be a connection between the two dreams. At any rate, Mrs. K. has had a terrible horror of fire all her life. So far, nothing involving a fire has happened to her in actual life, but she feels that her fear is based upon an earlier existence, with her childhood dream pointing to danger or perhaps death connected with fire.

JoAnne M. lives in Ohio and has never shown any interest in the occult or in reincarnation in particular. Two of her adolescent recurrent dreams have left her with a sense of fear to the point where she is still afraid to be alone in a two-story house at night. She also has a deep-rooted fear of knives.

She started having the first of the two dreams when she was about eight years old. In the dream, she is riding an old-model bike, perhaps the kind that was in use at the turn of the century or shortly thereafter. She sees herself riding in a park that has trees and a stream, and she is going down a hill. When she reaches the bottom of the hill, there is another hill but on the other side of the stream, which has a bridge across it. She crosses the bridge and on top of the second hill, she finds what seems to be a Victorian house, two-storied with many turrets, porches and gables. She dismounts from her bike and leaving it outside, enters the house. At this point in the dream, she always wakes up in terror with the certain knowledge that she was very much afraid inside the house in the dream.

Since she has this dream primarily when she is ill, there might be a connection between the inside of the house and illness.

The other dream she had during her early teens. At the time Mrs. M. and her sister shared a large dormer type bedroom in the attic of a bungalow. At one end of the room were their beds, at the other end the stairs that curved down to the main floor. She would often dream of an old lady ascending some stairs, with a huge knife in her hand and in the dream Mrs. M. knew that she was going to be stabbed. She would wake up terrified and would often lie awake for hours, staring at the stairs, waiting for the woman to come up, and afraid to go to sleep because she knew the woman would come. "I had this dream over and over and I would be terrified, lying in a cold sweat. I never told my mother or anyone else because I was in my teens and embarrassed that they would think I was odd," Mrs. M. explains. When she went on to college, the dream faded and she has never had it since.

But to this day she is afraid of knives, even small paring knives, in another person's hands. And whenever her husband is out of town, she is afraid to sleep alone in their second-story bedroom. She turns on all the lights, brings the dog into the room with her, and it is often early morning before she can finally fall asleep.

June Weidemann, a professional nurse, has long had an active interest in parapsychology. In her case this is not surprising since she has experienced a number of unusual incidents all her life. Again, she is one of the few people who combines ESP ability with some reincarnation dreams.

When June was seven years old she suddenly seemed to "wake up," and had a distinct feeling of being in a strange place with strange people. For a period of about six months she was convinced that her parents were not her parents at all because of their peculiar *round* eyes—which seemed strange to her. Finally, her mother had had enough, and showed her newspaper clippings announcing her birth, and her birth certificate, to convince her that she really was their daughter!

This did indeed convince June, but about that time she had a recurrent dream concerning a household compound in a house in China. All she could ever see was the bare compound laid with large, flat stones and a wall of the same material. In the center grew a tree which sometimes had beautiful blossoms and sometimes was bare and covered lightly with a layer of snow. There was no one else there but herself. At the same time she became aware of a certain perfume that surrounded her. This particular odor would always bring to mind the words "ming tree," although she did not at the time know what ming trees were. The oriental dream is rather comforting to Mrs. Weidemann, and in this life she has grown more and more fond of oriental things.

However, she has had two other recurrent dreams which are more disturbing. In one of them she is a young man with leather britches standing on top of a crude ladder that is leaning against a high wall. It is night; the ground below her falls away from the ladder, and she finds herself slowly falling backward, still holding tightly to the top rung of the ladder. She usually jerks herself awake with this dream, but sometimes, just before she hits the ground, she thinks to herself, still in the dream, "Oh no, not again!" The night is always dark, but there is moonlight or some other source of light, for she can see herself falling away from the wall and finds herself trapped under the ladder on the ground.

In still another dream she sees a house in the distance, and runs toward it, happy that she is home at last. She sees herself going up to a porch and she notices the long glass windows on each side of the door. She enters, but the house is bare. She steps down two steps into a room off the foyer.

There she sees a rather dilapidated staircase, and a long room with a bay window to the right. Occasionally, when she has had this dream, she has also seen antique furniture in the room, but mostly she sees a threadbare rug on the floor and an empty room. The dream ends there. She has never been in such a house in this life. The dream does not unduly upset her, as does the first one, where she falls off the ladder, and being a trained nurse and a well-read psychical researcher, Mrs. Weidemann has long since learned to cope with her reincarnation dreams.

HOW TO ENLARGE CONSCIOUSNESS THROUGH DREAMS

Granted that the dream state is one of dissociation of the conscious and unconscious minds, we need not wait for external forces to supply us with information or directives to benefit from this condition. Without interfering with, or replacing this external material, we can use the faculty of dreaming to enhance our personal accomplishments, our personality, even our health.

First, we can use the dream state to solve problems we have been unable to solve while awake. For instance, a test in school has puzzled us, or some unresolved situation has been on our minds when we went to sleep. We can program ourselves to find the solution in the dream state and to remember it upon awakening. This is done by gentle, persistent suggestion just prior to falling asleep, couching it in simple language and very few words, repeating the formula two or three times and then abandoning it. As soon as the suggestion is made to the unconscious, the dreamer must change the subject, so to speak, and think of something else, something totally disconnected from the desired dream action. Upon awakening, he/she will probably find the solution to the problem of the day before. This does not mean that the solution has been given by some external source, like an ancient *deus ex machina*, but simply that the solution was already in his/her unconscious at the time when he/she thought he/she did not have it. His/her dream condition merely awoke the slumbering giant and brought the information to his/her consciousness. Rather than running to the nearest Gypsy fortuneteller, most people would probably do better by consulting their own inner voice, carefully noting what they remember upon awakening. The unconscious reception center sees everything, hears everything, knows everything whereas, unfortunately, communication with the conscious level of the personality is another matter. By programming yourself to dream of the desired situation, you are in fact establishing a bridge to your own unconscious. The same technique can be used to recall the past, to remember forgotten material which is of interest to you, or even search for knowledge which you may possess but are not sure of, by simply programming yourself to dream of a specific period in your life. Edgar Cayce has recommended the dream state as an excellent way of tapping the "akashic records" and learning of one's earlier reincarnations. Similarly, some people will meditate just before bedtime so that they may learn of their prior lives while they are sleeping.

Healing body and mind is also possible in the dream state. Go over the ailment or problem just before bedtime, carefully pinpointing its causes and probable extent. Then visualize the ailment disappearing, and full health taking its place. After you have done so, program yourself to receive healing from universal sources while asleep, and go to bed with the positive attitude that healing will indeed take place. What you are doing is setting in motion the body and mind's own defense forces, while at the same time allowing the dream state to supply you with useful information concerning your health upon awakening.

You can develop a potential ESP capability by suggesting to your unconscious that the dream state be utilized to expand consciousness, and begin receiving material from external sources as well as from your unconscious, to be brought to the surface and remembered upon awakening. Eventually, if you do this on a regular basis, you will have ESP experiences that increase in time as you continue this technique.

Much was made some years ago of devices connected with earphones placed below the pillow so that the sleeper would be subjected to a low-keyed voice repeating certain words over and over. But learning in one's sleep has never been very successful. While it is true that in single cases suggestion made in this manner may reach the unconscious level exactly the way a human voice would, the method fails to work once the sleeper has reached the deeper levels of sleep and begins to dream.

The dream state can be of great use in advancing desired objectives, and there is a great range of topics, from success in careers to psychosexual fantasies. If you go to sleep with the firm intention of dreaming of a future accomplishment that you want to take place, you begin by visualizing it happening to you just as you drift off to sleep. In many instances, dream material will follow up on the suggestion you have made to your own subconscious, and you may indeed have a dream in which your wish comes true. It is even possible that astral projection will follow.

If the wish-dream involves another person, he/she may become aware of your dreaming. This awareness may take the form of a dream by the subject of your wishful dreaming or even a conscious awareness of what you're dreaming, even if there is a time difference between the two of you. As in other cases, here, too, astral projection may take place. In any event, no harm is done if there is a positive reaction to your dreams, nor is there any harm done if the other person is not aware that you have initiated the relationship. All that happens is that you yourself have a pleasurable experience.

Positive results will depend a great deal on conditions at the time of the dream and how it is received by any other person involved. Occasionally, dream projections have amazing results.

According to Dr. Stanley Krippner of the Maimonides Hospital Dream Laboratory in

Brooklyn, New York, the sleep state nowadays called REM, meaning rapid eye movement, is the period in which most remembered dreaming takes place. Dr. Wilse B. Webb, research psychologist at the University of Florida, says that an average of thirty-five sleep stage changes takes place during a single night, indicating quite a bit of wandering about by the dreamer in comparatively short periods. Of course, the number of dreams remembered upon awakening is a mere fraction of those which have actually occurred in the course of a night. As research initiated by Dr. Krippner continues, more is being learned concerning the nature of REM episodes during sleep. It appears that the rapid eye movement episodes occur at fairly regular intervals, primarily during the last third of the night, according to researchers Dr. W. C. Dement and Nathaniel Kleitman. They have also found that REM sleep occurs even in the daytime, not just during nighttime sleep.

In *The Sleep Book*, one of the best works dealing with dream and sleep, Shirley Motter Linde and Louis M. Savery have put together various theories, expressed in language understandable to the layperson.

The authors report that 65 per cent of ESP experiences reported to the Institute for Parapsychology in Durham, North Carolina occurred during the dream state. "If you find as you keep track of your dreams that you have premonitions of events to come or seem to pick up other people's thoughts, do not become alarmed; accept these experiences as an enhancement of your life, and use the dreams in whatever positive ways that suggest themselves," say the authors. They suggest a kind of exercise to deal with bad dreams after awakening. Close your eyes and think of the dream, vividly picturing the most frightening elements in it, then, consciously, make changes in the dream, befriending the horrors, as it were, and so gradually lessening their impact. This, of course, is useful only with non-message type dreams, but I shouldn't think it a good idea to dismantle veridical and paranormal dreams in this manner, since the essence of such dreams is to get a message through to the conscious mind, to have it accepted, and, in most cases, acted upon.

Katharine Cover Sabin (*ESP and Dream Analysis*) has an excellent suggestion concerning dream control. "The novice should begin his system of autosuggestion by pointing to the solar plexus area, and addressing the subconscious as follows: 'my dreams are becoming progressively more outstanding and predictive. I shall remember my dreams after I wake up.' These suggestions should be given at intervals during the day and upon retiring."

"Wake up to the enormous power of dreams," screams a newspaper advertisement for Dr. Ann Faraday's *The Dream Game*. Dr. Faraday, a psychologist, suggests that dreamers compile personal dream diaries and keep them up. On sexually oriented dreams, whether originated by the dreamer him/herself or the result of libido, she has this to say:

"All our energies have an erotic character; the drive toward reproductive sex is just one of many possible manifestations of the basic life urge to 'pour ourselves into,' or 'embrace' or 'take into ourselves' whatever excites us throughout the fibers of our being." In essence, what she is saying is that all wish fulfillment dreams, regardless of subject matter, are erotically tinged.

But Dr. Faraday also states, "Dreams that seem to give warnings of a more dramatic or paranormal nature come true only in a tiny minority of cases; for every uncanny story that is written up in the press, there are thousands of equally valid vivid dreams about friends dying, air crashes, floods, wars breaking out, or presidents being assassinated which are never literally fulfilled." Nothing could be further from the truth. Anyone truly familiar with the material on record will point out that the number of verified paranormal dreams is much greater than "a tiny minority," something in the nature of 25 per cent.

Why do *some* such dreams not come true as dreamt? To begin with, who is to say when the cutoff date is for such dream material? Many of the dreams concerning catastrophes, etc., may yet become objective reality in the future. Finally, where the cutoff date has already occurred because of the nature of the particular dream, it may well be that the dream was a warning dream to begin with, and the results had somehow been aborted. Certainly, there is a fraction of dreams which are false to begin with, and should be explained not on paranormal grounds but as expressions of a symbolic or strictly personal nature.

"It is common knowledge among parapsychological researchers that the great majority of reports which really do seem to show ESP involve incidents that are totally trivial in themselves," is another statement by Dr. Faraday which shows her lack of understanding of precognitive dreams. These seeming trivialities prove that paranormal dreaming is a quasi-mechanical operation and not selective as to the importance of material transmitted, as I have already pointed out. Just like Katharine Sabin, Dr. Faraday accepts symbolic ESP dreams, and is therefore able to say, "Many cases of real ESP may be missed when an image presents itself symbolically rather than literally—which all adds to the difficulty and confusion inherent in this field of research." There is no conclusion where I stand, and ESP material, as I have already stated several times in this book, need not be looked for in symbolic or otherwise confusing dreams; there is always clarity and a crisp to-the-point nature inherent in *true* paranormal dreams.

"People who have difficulty recalling dreams should try not to wake up too abruptly, but should lie in a passive and relaxed state for a moment or two," advises Tom Chetwynd in *How to Interpret Your Own Dreams*. His book, styled "an encyclopaedic dictionary" is little more than an alphabetical list of dream interpretations along "Babylonian" lines. It may be very useful for non-psychic dreams because it gives a wide range of potential interpretations of symbolisms encountered in dreams. But it is of no use with true paranormal dreams, which are messages in themselves and do not require "interpretations." Just so that this work is not mistaken for anything of a paranormal nature, the author states, "This is not a book of games, predictions, or other nonsciences," and it does contain 583 different dream subjects. Certainly, the book will come in handy as an adjunct to Tarot cards.

I can think of no better way of closing this chapter than to mention the work of Dr. John Mariani, Professor of Mathematics, a consultant scientist, member of the American Physical Society and the New York Academy of Sciences. Dr. Mariani has spent many years in research dealing with theoretical physics, and has been trying to explore the peculiar properties of space and time at subatomic levels. He has made some startling discoveries which are perhaps too technical to be included here in detail. Suffice it to say, however, that he began by noting the bizarre behavior of time under certain conditions, mentioned by Albert Einstein, according to which space and time could interchange each other suddenly. This means that time would also flow in reverse direction, that is, future to past, and not only in the conventional and accepted way, past to future. Dr. Mariani cites as an example a fast observer making a round trip around the earth, and having lived ten years, finding that the earth itself grew older by 100 years. "The gist of my theory, which is regarded as correct by other authorities," Dr. Mariani states, "is that these peculiar properties of space and time instead of being localized in sub-atomic levels as in usual theories, can in rare cases emerge at human level, giving rise, in my opinion, to those extraordinary phenomena usually regarded as "supernatural or miraculous," or simply denied. Also, space and time are not fundamental concepts but derive from an abstract formalism which does not retain anything of their intuitive aspects."

In short, what Dr. Mariani is working on may yet prove a perfectly rational, scientific basis for all paranormal behavior, and require a re-evaluation of our notions concerning time and space. Which is what I have been saying for many years, since I contend that we need not relegate psychic occurrences to positions *outside* conventional scientific concepts, but, to the contrary, adjust our scientific concepts to the *existing* facts and in doing so discover that they fit well within the new framework.

One of the cornerstones of orthodox scientific thinking has always been that time flows but in one direction. Dr. Mariani, and, I am sure, others in physics are in the process of proving otherwise. The ability to dream true would then no longer be regarded as an extraordinary phenomenon but a perfectly natural occurrence within the framework of our knowledge concerning the existing universe.

HOW TO
INTERPRET YOUR
OWN DREAMS

We all dream—every night—even though sometimes we do not seem to remember our dreams. There are four different types of dreams, really, and they mean quite different things. There is, first of all, the *anxiety dream*, where we find ourselves in a state of fear or upset, and which usually means that something we have not resolved in our waking condition, or not fully, keeps bothering us during our sleep when the conscious mind is not operating and the unconscious mind, the free and sometimes unrestrained part of our personality, has the power to impress us. Anxiety dreams are natural and normal parts of our daily lives and not necessarily an indication of illness or the need to spend long hours and much money with psychoanalysis, which, more often as not, does not really help resolve the underlying problems solving them in the real world, or adjusting to them does.

Typical anxiety dreams might include:

You are on a train or bus or airplane, or trying to catch one and being very worried about missing it. Or you are already on board but your luggage is not, or the luggage is and you are still outside worried about losing it. These dreams occur to many people from time to time and do not mean you are about to travel somewhere. Instead, the "train" (or bus or plane) means your ongoing life, your progress into the future, and the fear of not getting on or losing your luggage simply means you are concerned about your future security— whether work-wise or personal security. It is a very common dream.

Another dream often reported to me involves finding yourself "back in school" or in youth, at a time when you did not yet have full responsibility for yourself. On the one hand fear of not doing well in school would indicate basic insecurity with your work performance today; on the other hand, dreaming of a time when all was serene in your life, and your parents took care of your needs, is a deep desire not having to face up to present day difficulties in your life—sort of a dream escape into a simpler yesterday. A dream where the boss visits your house unexpectedly and you are thrilled by it, yet are also embarrassed about him finding you unprepared, would best be interpreted as your desire to want an advance on the job, ask for a raise perhaps, but being not sure whether you deserve it or if you should ask.

Falling from heights, sometimes accompanied by a sense of dizziness and usually followed by a state of tiredness on awakening, indicates a different type of dream, namely an *out-of-the-body experience*, and not a true dream at all. It occurs when the "traveler" returns from a faster-moving dimension (the astral) and gets back "in" the physical body-shell again, which moves at a slower speed, therefore the sensation of slowing down expressed in this falling experience. People have done astral travel for thousands of years, sometimes reporting events or people at a distance they think they "dreamed" about when in fact their spirit bodies were actually seeing these events or people and remembering them on awakening. Astral projections or out of the body experiences are common and not in the least harmful other than a little tiredness after awakening: but then all travel tires one, after all.

There is a kind of dream, better perhaps called a *nightmare*, which is caused by physical discomfort or illness of the body. Nightmares can be triggered by anything from a cold and fever, to indigestion, to being too hot or too cold in bed. Or it can be caused by having earlier witnessed a horror movie or a real accident—anything that would have been frightening in real life and usually not long before the nightmare comes on. Obviously, if you dream of monsters devouring you, or being done some kind of violence, such as being in a shipwreck, or drowning in the ocean, or being pursued by anything ranging from murderous people to demons and devils with horns, you are having a nightmare. Frequently it also involves a kind of pressure on your chest—the very name "nightmare" derives from the old superstitious belief that such dreams were caused by an invisible horse sitting on your chest!

Truly bizarre dreams of this kind should not be taken seriously as anything other than what they are and if you search your memory as to what you experienced the day before, you will find the explanation for what has caused your unconscious mind to react so violently. Your unconscious is pure emotion and cannot reason things out, so the monsters are real on that level. On the other hand, eating heavily within two hours before bedtime can easily cause such dreams as can a variety of fever-connected illnesses. There are also some medically prescribed drugs, from stimulants to painkillers to tranquilizers that can cause such wild, irrational dream images. None of this represents anything permanent or dangerous.

Finally, there is a fourth category of dreams, wherein you experience something of a psychic nature. The *psychic dream*, which is always remembered after awakening and for long periods (contrary to all the other dreams) can be of two kinds: a warning in the form of a premonition or projection of danger ahead (which can then be avoided) or simply a prophetic dream in which you foresee future events clearly as part of your own ESP ability—not exactly uncommon. When you do have a psychic dream, always check whether you are the outside observer of events or actually in the picture. If you are outside, chances are it is a warning and not final, but if you are in the "film" better take heed and be careful.

There is also a relatively rare experience of dreaming of a past life: if it is truly that, it will be very specific in details of place, time and names, and will become a *recurrent dream* with little change in the scenario. Such experience can be followed up through hypnotic regression, which I have done in valid cases with frequent success, to widen the information where it can actually be verified from research sources.

We have come a long way from simplistic dream interpretation, whether Sigmund Freud's sexually-tinged way of explaining all dreams, or the other extreme, Gypsy fortunetellers' ridiculous and often frightening ways of claiming meanings without validity.

We all dream and we all have the ability to interpret what "comes up" when we do. By learning to distinguish between these various and very different types of dreams, we can understand ourselves better and profit from possible warnings or glimpses into the future.

DREAM SYMBOLS
& CATEGORIES

In this chapter we will examine the main categories of dreams, what they mean, and how they can he usefully employed in a practical sense, far beyond the use psychoanalysis has put them to. In addition, there will be a section dealing with the more usual kinds of dreams and dream symbols, and what they may mean to the dreamer.

Dr. Sigmund Freud discovered the value of dreams in interpreting a person's emotional state, a notion that was extremely ill received at the time by his peers in the medical profession. Until the late 19th century, dreams had been considered the result of physical discomfort or of emotional turmoil at best, but their value as a tool to determine the mental health of a person had not yet been discovered.

People who spoke of the importance of dreams in terms of understanding the psyche were usually considered quacks or romanticists who had somehow mistaken the poetic notion that one's dreams may come true at times for the hard facts of dream interpretation. It remained for Dr. Freud to offer a totally new concept of the significance of dreams.

Freud offered nothing less than the theory that our repressed emotions manifest in dreams, and that the analysis of dream material could yield valuable keys to the understanding of human nature. It is well known that this new theory was received with great disdain by the medical profession, almost ending Freud's promising career as a physician. Somehow, however, he overcame his adversaries and in the end he triumphed.

Freud, the "father of psychoanalysis," was the undisputed master of the unconscious until one of his most promising pupils, Dr. Carl Jung of Zurich altered the concept considerably, putting less stress on sexual symbolism in dreams, and more on what Jung called archetypes, thus creating a somewhat different path for the understanding of humankind through dreams. In addition to Freud and Jung, there are of course others who have contributed toward the development of psychoanalysis, from Adler to Reik and from Karen Horney to Newman.

Countless books deal with psychoanalysis in its various forms, and according to its various schools, from medical texts to popular handbooks, and it is not the intention, nor is it the province, of this book to deal with them from that point of view. To the contrary, this book offers an alternate route to the understanding of dreams, without wishing to abolish or suggesting the abolition of traditional psychoanalytical approaches in *some* cases. What I'm offering is a more complete picture of the importance of dreams, because I am convinced that the psychoanalytical-psychiatric evaluation of dreams does not take into account the psychic climate in dreams, without realizing perhaps that precisely that element is a major factor in dreaming, and must consequently be included in any kind of evaluation of dream material, whether the evaluator agrees with the findings of parapsychology or not.

On the other end of the spectrum, there are equally as many so-called Gypsy dream books, written not necessarily by Gypsies in the literal sense of the term, but by people who take their scientific responsibilities toward proper dream interpretation somewhat lightly. Frequently, such books cross the line from non-fiction to fiction, and while some of them are amusing and others interesting, the majority is nothing more than pulp literature, bereft of any serious value to the one using it.

Conversely, I feel that a simple glossary of the more common forms of dreams with their significance as seen from the point of view of an all-inclusive interpretation, one that takes into account traditional evaluation as well as the psychic side, might benefit those using this work. And it is with that in mind that the following material is offered. No attempt at completeness is being made, for there are as many variations of human dreams as there are humans in existence;

on the other hand, it will be found that certain dreams follow distinctive and specific patterns, and by altering one or the other term or symbolism or imagery one can arrive at parallel dreams with pretty much the same factors involved and thus use differing dreams under headings referring to parallel material, even if the dream material discussed is not identical with the one one wishes to have examined.

There will, of course, be gray areas, material that lies between one and the other category or class of dream material, then several categories must be examined in order to arrive at some sort of conclusion. Nothing is firm when it comes to the evaluation of dream material, because *similar* dreams occurring to different people may signify *different* things. Unfortunately, I have not as yet become convinced that dreams mean the same thing at all times to all dreamers, even identical dreams do not. If, as I have postulated, being adream, or asleep, is merely a state of consciousness and not an action in itself, then there is plenty of room for *variable* results deriving from *identical* dream experiences, and any kind of blanket interpretation becomes *impossible*.

With all that in mind, I am nevertheless offering the following material in the hope that it will prove useful to some, if not all.

Accidents

When you dream of an accident happening to you, it could be a psychic warning dream, and you should always consider it as such in taking certain precautions. But accident dreams can also indicate fear of accidents, to the point where they represent unusual anxieties caused perhaps by insecurities of one kind or another, such as fear that one is not a good enough driver, fear that crossing the street is dangerous, fear that one is not in full control over one's movements. Unless an accident dream is of a genuine psychic nature and represents a warning, chances expresses an inborn anxiety about one's prowess, a lack of confidence in one's physical coordination.

Animals speaking

Talking dogs or cats in dreams, since obviously they do not do so in real life, represent unexpressed feelings about such animals. This type of dream is much more common, for obvious reasons, with animal owners, but it has also occurred to those who do not have a pet in their home. In most cases the dream represents a transference of an opinion to be expressed by a human being into the mouth of an animal, thus making it at one time miraculous and below one's, or anyone's, station. A human speaking the same sentence would have to be replied to, but if an animal speaks, it does so to serve the master and one is not responsible for this to the same degree.

Birds

Nearly all civilizations pay special attention to dreams involving birds, whether single birds or entire flocks. Birds were thought to be lucky and prophetic at the same time, and the Romans were very much interested in the number of birds one dreamed about, the directions they came from or went to, even the angle the bird descended to earth. Unless the dreamer is aware of these ancient interpretations and they are part of his/her personal beliefs, I should think that bird dreams represent nothing more than an unconscious desire to be "as free as a bird," to be able to take off at will and to travel very fast. Such dreams would indicate frustrations and impatience with one's current conditions, dislike of being unable to move as freely as the unconscious desires.

Boss visiting

A dream involving an unexpected visit by the boss indicates two things: on the one hand it indicates that such an idea is totally unacceptable to the dreamer in the wakeful state, on the other hand it implies a fear that the boss might find things not to his/her liking, should he/she choose to visit the home of the dreamer. This type of dream would indicate an anxiety situation toward the employer, caused perhaps by feelings of inadequacy or knowledge that all is not as it should be on the job.

Butterflies

Just as with birds, butterflies have held a special place in the poetic fantasy world of the ancients. On the other hand, dreaming of butterflies would indicate an identification with nature, the free world of the woods, the ability to move about freely and yet slowly. Butterflies also imply things of beauty unimpeded by the ugliness of reality, such as having to earn a living. Thus butterfly dreams should be categorized as unexpressed desires for greater freedom.

Cemeteries

Despite some popular misconceptions and superstitions, dreaming of cemeteries does not imply imminent death by the dreamer or someone close to him. Unless the cemetery dream is specific and has psychic elements in it, it would appear to indicate an unconsciously expressed link with past generations, whether in terms of family or in terms of country of origin. Cemeteries therefore do not signify so much the gravestones as the traditions of the past and the desire to recognize them, to acknowledge them and to continue whatever it is one's ancestors have started. People who have dreams of cemeteries are generally searching for identity in their national or even racial existence, and far from being depressing, cemetery dreams are actually reminders of one's proud ancestry.

Christ

Depending upon the dreamer's religious orientation, a father figure appearing in the dream looking very much like the traditional image of Jesus Christ would indicate a greater need for religious expression, which the dreamer somehow feels he/she has not fulfilled. Leaving out as far-fetched possibility that the literal Jesus Christ visits dreamers in their sleep state, although we cannot prove this, there remains the symbolic significance of such an illustrious dream visit. Christ represents the symbolic religious expression of humans, but also their suffering on behalf of that expression. Dreams involving the Christ therefore should be interpreted as a need for a greater identification with the religious world one is born into or has adopted, and a symbolic rejection of the more material aspects of one's past behavior.

Dead people

Another superstition which has no basis in fact concerns the dream visit by dead relatives or friends. In some Eastern European and Southern European cultures this is believed to signify that the dreamer or someone close to him will soon be taken away by the visiting dead person and that the visit is in the nature of a preparation to acquaint the dreamer with impending doom. In this respect such dreams tie up with the Irish concept of the banshee, and similar concepts in other cultures of death warnings, such as blackbirds or unexplained strong noises at the door or window. But the appearance of the dead, if not truly psychic visitations, would indicate a symbolic need to link back with them, if they are relatives or close friends, and a rejection by the dreamer of reality. Insufficiency of friendship or recognition by the living could also be cited as the cause why the dead appear in such dreams. But it should be noted that a large percentage of such dreams do indicate psychic communications.

Death personified

When the dreamer recognizes Death as a person, looking anything from the traditional skeleton or the man in black to a forbidding angel, he/she is exteriorizing the concept which represents finality, and thus fear. Again, the dream of Death as a person does not necessarily indicate impending death for the dreamer or someone close to him/her, but may very well indicate the end of a concept in the dreamer's life; symbolically it expresses a fear of something coming to an end, and the inability of the dreamer to accept this consciously and realistically.

Desert, alone in

A fairly common anxiety dream involves being left alone in the desert, usually without water, and trying to get out or get help. Here the dreamer symbolizes his/her loneliness and the sense of frustration that no one cares; he/she is trying to reach out, only to find that he is alone in the desert of disinterest on the part of his/her fellow humans.

Faceless double

Faceless doubles, men or women appearing to walk at exactly the same rate of speed as oneself, but never close enough to be recognized, are a common occurrence in dreams. The double represents a part of the person's own unconscious, the part that he/she is not too familiar with or the part that he/she cannot control. Whatever he/she does, the faceless double acts simultaneously, yet the dreamer is unable to reach out and touch the double or to blend to make a whole. Faceless double type dreams indicate a lack of integration in the dreamer's personality, and inability to cope with present problems by fully utilizing the self in all its aspects, and with all its capacities.

Falling from heights

Falling from heights nearly always indicates the end of an astral projection dream, an out-of-the-body experience. Occasionally, however, falling from heights, especially when it is an *actual* mountaintop or other high point, may indicate something else, such as the fear of heights, agoraphobia, or a condition in the dreamer's personality because of which he/she is unable to attain a goal. Falling from heights then symbolizes his/her very real fear of stumbling at the last moment when reaching out for the higher goal, and it represents a lack of confidence in accomplishing what he/she wants.

Funerals

Just like dreams of death and of visitations by the dead, dreams of funerals do not necessarily indicate that one is imminent. If the funeral dream is not of a psychic nature, that is to say if it does not indicate a specific individual who is about to die, and is merely a dream of funerals *in general*, it would indicate a symbolic fear of life's end for the dreamer, a depressed outlook, perhaps even an unconscious desire to leave the physical world through death's door in order to escape the struggle for survival.

God

Just as with dreams in which Jesus Christ appears to the dreamer, dreams of God, where God appears as a person, are a symbolic reflection of the dreamer's own need for religious recognition and paternal protection. The God image then becomes the authority that dispenses justice in what to the dreamer is an unfair condition in real life. Dreams in which God appears do not necessarily mean that the dreamer is about to be summoned before the throne of the deity, but would indicate to the contrary that the dreamer appeals symbolically to judgment, an adjustment of his/her condition on earth, and at the same time a reaffirmation of his/her own religious faith. Thus a very positive kind of dream.

Hole in the ground

The hole-in-the-ground image represents fear of stumbling in one's daily existence, of unexpected difficulties, unexpected hindrances into which one may disappear. Rarely does such a dream represent a real hole, but must be taken symbolically as inability by the dreamer to reconcile him/herself with potential hazards along the road to success.

Letter arriving

Dreams in which a letter arrives, usually bringing unexpected news, are very common; in some cases they actually represent a precognitive experience concerning a real letter which arrives sometimes a day, sometimes much later, but a fair percentage of such dreams have no precognitive connotation at all and must be explained symbolically. The desire to have news is a very real motivating force in such dreams, and proves that the dreamer would like an alteration of his condition through news from an external source. Thus the dream of a letter arriving represents a wish fulfillment expression of the unconscious, not necessarily a real letter. The letter is merely the symbol of some sort of action, some sort of news that would change things for the dreamer.

Money

Any dream in which money appears, whether hard currency or paper money or a letter containing money or news of money, reflects one of two unconscious symbolisms. On the one hand it may indicate a need to see one's efforts crowned by financial recognition, this not being the case in reality at the time. On the other hand, money, as a symbolic expression of freedom, may indicate the dreamer's expressed desire to be free from some of the things he/she has to do in order to earn money. Despite popular superstitions, dreaming of money doesn't mean that money is about to arrive, and while it does indicate a preoccupation of the dreamer with the subject, it would indicate to me that dreaming of money is just that and nothing more. One should remember that money represents freedom from drudgery as well as purely financial power and such dreams should be understood in terms of individual freedom rather than financial accumulations.

Nakedness, embarrassing

When the dream contains a situation in which the dreamer finds him/herself naked, among people who are not, thus creating an embarrassing situation for the dreamer, we are faced with an expressed symbolism involving fear of being naked. The nakedness then represents helplessness in the company of those who are powerful. It may also, to a lesser degree, represent hang-ups concerning the body, in cases where the dreamer is less than satisfied with his or her appearance.

Numbers

Dreaming of certain numbers has always held fascination for people, because it occurred to most dreamers that it indicated help from "above" to win money in some sort of lottery. Thus, the most immediate reaction by dreamers when they remember having dreamt certain numbers is to put them into the nearest lottery game, frequently without the slightest success. Dreaming of numbers, unless it is a specific number which has immediate significance in terms of recognition, may symbolize the idea of counting, that is to say organizing one's life, taking stock of assets and liabilities. Numbers may also indicate dates, of course, and no general rule for the significance of dreaming of numbers can really be given. Only a fraction of number dreams are truly psychic in nature. When remembering dreams dealing with numbers, one should be aware of the generic nature of figures, and not necessarily seek symbolism in a particular number but consider such dreams as dealing with the symbolic process of counting and numbering.

Running, not moving

A dream in which the dreamer attempts desperately to run, presumably to run away from some unseen or unknown danger, but finds him/herself unable to move from the spot is not uncommon. It represents a suppressed fear that one is unable to escape from an unpleasant situation, despite trying to do so. This kind of anxiety dream shows that the dreamer is unable to make realistic preparations for certain situations that may occur in his life, or finds himself unable to cope with a situation from which he/she wishes to escape.

School, being back in

A fairly common dream of adults is finding themselves back in school all of a sudden, going back many years in some instances, with the impression that one has to do a certain task or obey certain rules, with all the implied anxieties. Dreams showing oneself back in school are in actuality masking real life situations on the job or in one's professional life, which are not as they should be. As one fears being back in school and being responsible for performing certain tasks the teacher expects, one shifts a similar situation from the reality of the work day into the fantasy world of being out of place as an adult, back in school. Such dreams should be examined in the light of one's current problems, if any, on the job.

Sexual dreams

Probably the most controversial (but also the most interesting) of all dream symbolisms are the various sexual dreams, which do not necessarily always mean what they appear to indicate.

Firstly, if you dream of having sexual intercourse with a desirable partner, the meaning will depend on the state of your own position in reality. If you know the person who is your dream partner, but are not likely to have intercourse with him/her, your dream would indicate a wish fulfillment/escape syndrome and as such easily lead to a state of depression, despite its upbeat content.

If the dream appears to be between yourself and an unknown partner, or someone whom you cannot recognize, it would indicate dissatisfaction with your existing relationship. If the dream represents you in a much more favorable light as a sexual partner than you feel yourself to be in reality, it might indicate a sense of insecurity in sexual matters. You compensate in the dream state for what you think you cannot attain in the wakeful condition.

When your dream imagery tends to become extreme in its sexual connotations, such as with orgies, sadomasochistic elements and other bizarre forms of sex, you will have to find an interpretation in your own sexual makeup elements of which may be under the surface, not even in your conscious mind. the unconscious is telling you something about yourself you either don't realize or don't wish to know.

Sexual dreams can be real and quasi-three-dimensional to the point of reaching orgasm in the dream state; but they do not have the same release qualities wakeful sexual fantasies have, as if they are only secondhand stories rather than first person experiences.

Some sexual dreams are not as explicit or direct as the ones just mentioned, but are hidden in symbolism or expressed (by the unconscious) through parallel imagery. It is a form of skirting the issue not unlike the polite person who "goes to the bathroom" rather than the toilet.

Dreams in which snakes are prominent indicate fascination with the male libido; dreams in which circles, round objects, fruit, balls, or other spheric objects appear often refer to the female libido.

Being overpowered and seized by a stronger individual (usually of the opposite sex) denotes hidden desires to be on the receiving end of a sexual adventure.

Many people are able to express their sexual appetites consciously, frequently by using what is considered offensive or at least prurient language publicly. Some cannot do this by reason of upbringing or character traits inhibiting such behavior, but they may wish to express themselves in this manner nevertheless, and often do so in the dream state. Such dreams usually see the dreamer doing or saying things he/she would "never" do or say in real life and frequently shocks them as being alien to their nature, which it really isn't. When explicit sexual acts occur in dreams by people normally behaving in very inhibited or conservative fashion, it indicates a personality conflict in need of exteriorizing, perhaps with the result that a middle-of-the-road approach to sexual matters results.

Having illicit sex with a forbidden partner (such as incest, under-age relationships, homosexual relationships, sodomy, etc.) is not necessarily an indication of a "sick" psyche. It may mask a desire for sexual change of a much more conventional nature, expressed, however, in this exaggerated manner in order to catch the attention of the conscious mind.

Another category of sexual dreams has the dreamer view or experience sexual aspects or attributes of otherwise ordinary objects, such as buildings, cars, jewelry. The dreamer "sees" sexual connotations in everything around him/her, and projects such attributes where none should exist in reality. These are dreams in which the dreamer expresses his/her need for stronger sexual identity, but realizes he/she is prevented from expressing his/her true desires by restricting factors, such as society, church, moral code, et.

Lastly, sexual dreams in which sex organs appear to be out of all normal proportions as part of a sequence, indicate a fear of inadequacy thus compensated in this manner. In normal, fully adjusted dreamers, sex dreams are relaxing and pleasurable and mere extensions or anticipations of real life situations.

Dreaming of sex organs, sexual intercourse, nudity, etc. are of course in no way evil or "sinful" in terms of religion; their absence would indicate lack of interest in natural relationships and one would have to look for compensatory behavior elsewhere.

Ships

Dreaming of ships represents both symbolic meaning and actuality. In many civilizations, the ship is the representative of good fortune, for the sails of Fortuna are filled by the wind of good luck. Thus if one dreams of ships one may indeed dream of desired fortunes, expressing a need for intervention in one's real life by some external forces, to change one's luck. But a dream involving ships may also indicate a need to move forward, although slowly, since ships sail on the water, and do not move very fast. Thus the symbolism of a ship, especially the sailing ship, should be read as an indication of measured forward movement, or a need, expressed by the unconscious, for better fortunes.

Snakes

Dreams involving snakes, especially the venomous kind, are fear dreams in which the dreamer expresses horror at being surrounded by conditions from which he/she cannot escape. The snake then represents a cunning adversary, who may hold power over the dreamer. Dreams of snakes also indicate a fear by the dreamer of anything that moves in a hidden way, of powers he/she cannot counter or cope with.

Trains and cars

A very common category of dreams involves trains, that is to say missing trains or cars, running after them or getting on and not getting off at the right stop. This very common anxiety dream literally can be torture; the dreamer runs after the train as it pulls out of the station, or he/she gets on and his/her luggage is left behind or the dreamer is on board only to discover that he/she cannot leave the train at a particular stop because the doors are locked, or because he/she has forgotten to get up. The dream is fairly simple to analyze: trains (and, to a lesser degree, cars) represent life and movement, progress and the passage of time; the dreamer fears missing the train or not getting off at the right stop, meaning the dreamer is unsure of his/her position in the stream of life, and his/her unconscious is not reassuring ultimate achievements. People with this type of dream should examine their position, their professional abilities in relation to their accomplishments and outlook, and adjust them to the realities as they exist.

Turtle

In the Orient, dreaming of turtles meant longevity because the character for turtle in Chinese and Japanese is the same as the one meaning 10,000 years; but more than that, turtles represent longevity because they move so slowly and are tough and seem to be able to suffer all kinds of vicissitudes yet live to ripe old ages, not necessarily 10,000 years, but hundreds of years. Dreaming of turtles has always meant good luck. Thus the turtle image appears on medallions and decorations and signifies good fortune.

Unable to move

This anxiety dream in which the dreamer is fully aware of the need to make a move but unable to do so, and finds him/herself paralyzed and aware of it, is still another form of the common anxiety dream, representing suppressed fears: underachievement or that accomplishments will not be acknowledged by superiors. The inability to move, which characterizes this dream, is the dreamer's unconscious fear that he/she will not be able to make the right move.

Visits

Dream visits by unexpected relatives or friends do not necessarily reflect the actual visits the following day or in the near future, although there are a number of such dreams which are precognitive in nature, especially when the visitor is clearly recognized in a dream not easily forgotten upon arising. But the majority of such dreams seem to indicate something else; the dreamer desires to be visited by others, because he/she feels isolated and the dream visits indicate an existing link with others, relatives and friends, something he/she has somehow not been able to bring off in real life.

Weddings

Dreaming of weddings does not necessarily mean that the dreamer will get married, because a lot of married people also dream of weddings. The symbolism of the wedding dream lies in the joyful connotation which weddings imply, at least most of them at the outset, and should be taken as the unconscious expression of union with the partner, better relationship with the partner, whether a marriage or business, and an expression by the unconscious of a need for joining up, a need to be loved and respected. Once in a while, people dream of weddings, seeing details and even dates. and the weddings do take place; such dreams are of course psychic in nature.

PERSONAL ACCOUNTS & CASE STUDIES

Dreams are the telegraph of the unconscious mind.

We are either awake or adream rather than asleep, because the dream state is the other half of our living existence. Many people feel they don't dream because they can't remember their dreams on awakening, but I am convinced all of us dream every moment while we sleep, thus I prefer the term "adream" to "asleep."

As I stated in previous chapters, there are four types of dreams: the physical dream causing nightmares because of illness or bodily problems, the symbolic dream reflecting suppressed feelings, desires and problems (used in psychoanalysis), the psychic or clairvoyant dream transcending the boundaries of time and space, and out-of-the-body experiences in which the inner self leaves the physical body and travels, while observing people and things outside.

The first two categories are usually dealt with by psychiatrists and psychologists, the third and fourth however are the province of the parapsychologist like myself. In the clairvoyant dream, the sleeper is fully aware of the message or content, yet does not wake from the experience until it is over. On awakening, however, he/she remembers the dream very clearly and for long periods, which is not the case with the first two dream types. A good example comes from one of my readers in the *National Examiner*, Carolyn S. in Oklahoma. On July 6th, 1979 she went to sleep in the normal manner.

"I was sleeping," she writes, "when I heard the screaming sound of a siren and I dreamt I looked out the window, to see a big, black hearse drive down the street and stop in front of a large brick building. The driver and his attendant got out and opened the two back doors of the hearse. I wondered who had died and if I should notify someone.

"At that point, I awakened and it was so real that I jumped from bed and went outside to see if I could observe anything. I didn't, so went back to sleep.

"The next morning my mom called to tell me that my aunt had passed away that night in the hospital."

Dreams can leap across time barriers.

Rosanna Rogers is a well-known professional Tarot reader and psychic making her home in Cleveland, Ohio. Thousands of people have come to her to find out what the future has in store for them, and Rosanna has always had some word of truth. I myself have had readings with her that truly dazed me. But it never occurred to Rosanna that some day she would be the recipient of a dream vision concerning her own life. It happened on February 12, 1978, when she had just lay down for a nap. She saw herself in a hospital, apparently in a foreign country, for she could not understand the language easily, and she noticed that the beds in the crowded ward were put together with heads facing away from each other, but footends touching. In a bed standing along the wall she noticed a woman, but she could not recognize her face. In another bed she saw a man whom she knew well in the dream, and she knew he was dying.

Next to the hospital ward Rosanna noticed a kind of office filled with women, and she turned to them to report the death of the man in the bed. But the doctor whom she addresses is unable to understand her. Finally, one of the women in the room explains the situation, and at this point Rosanna felt great warmth and pity for the man who had just died.

The dream very much disturbed the Cleveland psychic, and she discussed it with a close friend. Cutting her own Tarot cards, she saw the so-called "death cards" all over her reading.

The following day, her sister burst in with a letter just received from Europe. Their mother had advised them she was suffering and asked for help. Five days later, Rosanna walked into the hospital of her dream: everything was exactly as she had seen it in her vision, even the position of the beds. The room full of women also turned out to have been correct. After a few days, Rosanna decided to check on her father whom she had not heard from in 33 years. She and her sister found him in a hospital, and again the bed was precisely the way Rosanna had seen it in her dream.

Both of her parents died within days of one another, but her father never recognized her prior to his passing.

Had Rosanna's dream been a way to prepare her for the double loss?

Can a dream mask wishful thinking and fantasy?

Not every dream is significant either as a symbolic expression of inner turmoil or unresolved issues, or as a psychic revelation with immediate significance to the dreamer or those around him. Some dreams may merely be vehicles of exteriorized fantasies which the dreamer is too shy or inarticulate to voice in the waking condition.

Sometimes it is difficult to say whether we are dealing with a fantasy dream or a real psychic dream, especially when the subject is a well-known personality. A good case in point was reported by one of my readers, Josephine W. of Pennsylvania.

"I had a dream the other night," she explained, "I went to see Elvis Presley's grave and it had dead flowers on it and I said to my mother 'How awful,' and I got a chill; it was in July and I looked at his mother's grave , and there was Elvis and his mother, they looked so young. He said, 'I'm not *here*, I'm happy, tell everyone I'm happy, leave me in peace.' I started to cry and he went to touch my cheek and I woke up."

Josephine wonders if it means she is turning "religious" or whether Elvis is trying to tell the world something through this dream.

Well, lots of people wish the singer were still alive down here, and of course this may only be a wish fulfillment dream. On the other hand, I once investigated the amazing case of a New Jersey housewife, Dorothy Sherry, who had visitations from Elvis Presley which contained a great deal of evidential material about his private life, not known to outsiders. The result of Dorothy's out-of-the-body experiences with Elvis Presley became a book, *Elvis Presley Speaks*.

Dozens of people all over the world say they have head from Elvis Presley since his passing. Some may be having fantasies, others are truly recipients of genuine messages from the singer who was always very much interested in the occult while in the flesh. It is conceivable that he has seen fit to continue his work with psychics from "over there," and Josephine's dream may very well belong in that category. Elvis apparently likes to use "amateur psychics" for his messages, rather than commercial soothsayers, on the theory that ordinary people are more likely to be believed.

What does it mean when you dream of water?

Sometimes a dream may use symbolic language to convey a message or idea to the sleeper. The unconscious mind, which is "in charge of" dreaming, is not always capable of expressing a thought in a straightforward fashion, and often surrounds a dream image with symbolic matter, or uses a code to express an idea. It is a moot point why this is so: whether it is simply the result of the human dream machine and a result of going through the unconscious level, or whether this is a karmic law to make us *work* at understanding the dream material, the fact is we should look at dreams not only for what they tell us in actual images, but also for the deeper meanings behind those images which may contain the real message.

Mrs. Vera O.C. of Wisconsin has a long record of clairvoyant dreams to her credit. Despite the fact some think her odd, she has dreamt "true" many times, such as when she dreamt that the earth beneath their trailer had caved in as she opened the door. A few days after the dream, a storm caused the earth around their pumphouse to cave in. Mrs. C. also has "waking flashes" when she sees things happening at a distance. Her sister-in-law appeared to her in a red automobile and instantly Mrs. C. knew that she was in danger. Her husband would not take her seriously, but several hours later they learned that the woman had been in an accident at the time of the vision.

But most of Mrs.C's dreams are about water: rivers, pools, lakes, bridges, bridges she cannot get across, sometimes alone, sometimes with people she knows , but the common factor is they cannot cross over the water for some reason. In one dream she is the only one who can cross safely, but on condition she take orders from someone she cannot see in the dream.

Water represents the flow of human tide, that is, life itself, and bridges over water symbolize difficulties and uncertainties. Mrs.C's anxieties (perhaps over being accepted by her family as a true psychic) are expressed in such dreams; the unseen person who gives the orders represents the higher order, God, destiny, etc., whatever caused her to be "different." But I don't think her water dreams represent real water, or dangers from water.

A Kennedy dream come true.

A reader in Virginia had an extraordinary dream or rather sequence of dreams which seem to defy the ordinary laws of time and space. Not that this is an isolated instance for her by any means: dreaming "true" is part and parcel of her daily life. She has taken her special gift in her stride, however, and knows she is a privileged person.

At the time when John F. Kennedy, still a Senator, was running for president, the woman was an active campaign worker, the only time in her life she had ever become involved in political work. She had never met the candidate, but felt his goals sufficiently worthwhile to help with the campaign on a local level. About that time she had a series of extraordinary dreams, all the same night.

In the first dream she saw herself enter a large room through an open door, with the feeling she had been chosen for a particular task. There was a desk with an empty chair in front of it. But a man was seated on the corner of the desk, he seemed very relaxed and smiled at her. He was dressed in a black suit and white shirt, his tie was black and white. As his legs were crossed, she noticed that he also wore white socks, but black shoes. That man was the later President Kennedy. As she observed, Kennedy turned his head and looked toward the other side of the room. There was a woman there, Mrs. Kennedy, seemingly suspended in mid-air, and dressed in sheer black which was billowing and blowing around her like clouds. She looked at Kennedy, both smiled and nodded their heads as if in secret agreement, then both looked at the dreamer. At that point, the woman from Virginia awoke.

After she went back to sleep, she found herself back in the same room, which was now dark where it had been sunlit before. Waking up again, the dreamer went back to sleep a third time. This time she found herself in a different room. A well-dressed man in his thirties was guiding her around the large room, and, to her surprise, she noticed the President's mother seated at a desk. She was then led to another desk and made to understand that it was for her, the dreamer. At that point, the dream ended.

Several years later, the woman saw Kennedy when he stopped in her town while campaigning. She stood close to his plane, Kennedy smiled at her, and came toward her with outstretched hand. But something made her run away from the handshake, and as she looked back toward the President, she saw once again the billowing black she had seen in her dream!

Dream or astral projection?

R.W. of Merced, California knows that life does not end at death's door. One morning in October, 1978, R.W. woke from a dream with tears in his eyes. The dream was so vivid it seemed like a real experience. In it, the dreamer was walking on Central Street in Los Angeles, when she saw her dead mother standing in the street, wearing the identical white dress the family had buried her in. In her hand, she had a Bible. R.W. ran to greet her, saying, as if nothing had happened, "Mother, where are you going?" The dead mother replied, "To church," and R.W. then introduced her husband and a friend who was with them, but the dead mother only replied, "You should pray, pray, pray!"

A second later, she began to lean to one side and it occurred to R.W. that her mother had had a leg amputated prior to her passing. In the next moment, the figure just melted into the ground.

For a moment after the dream had ended, R.W. stayed in bed, trying to figure out its meaning. Then something made her get up and walk across the hall to her brother-in-law's room. She found him unconscious, and though she managed to get him to a hospital quickly, he died shortly afterwards.

Evidently the realistic dream had been a warning of the passing. Such apparitions are not uncommon, especially among older families, such as the Irish, who call the "announcer" of death in the family, a banshee. In the case of R.W. however, it would appear that a materialization may have taken place and that she was in fact in the street when she spoke to her mother. Through astral projection, or out-of-the-body flight, a psychic person can accomplish this seemingly incredible feat.

The "dead" like to project themselves in the clothes they wore when they pass on, or at least in some easily recognizable way, which is possible as they are truly thought projections of their former physical bodies, and can appear the way they wish to appear if they can visualize themselves in that way.

Dreams can prevent accidents.

Terrena F. wonders about her odd feelings that things might happen to her—and they usually do. Like the time she was playing basketball in high school. As she was preparing for the game, she had the uneasy feeling that something might happen to her during the game, but of course she had no way to prevent it. Sure enough, during the ball game, another player's knee hit hers, causing it to pop out of joint. These "feelings" occur frequently, she explains, wondering if she has ESP—she does. But not all precognitive feelings are so vague that you can't do anything about them.

"One night not more than six weeks ago, I had a dream. My sister and I were in our car, a Mercury, and we were on our way to the college I attended, to pick up a friend. As we were getting off the exit, we hit a yellow Volkswagen. That was the end of the dream. After a day or two, I thought no more of the dream.

"A week later, I had gone to pick up this same friend. He and I were going to the movies. As we approached a shopping center, a yellow Volkswagen pulled out in front of us, and we barely missed hitting it."

Unquestionably, recognizing the image of her precognitive dream made Terrena act more quickly, thus preventing what might have been a tragic accident.

Some psychic dreams foretell future events exactly as they later occur: others are only warnings of what might happen if the dreamer fails to heed the warning.

Do dreams of celebrities have real meaning?

I have in my files a number of statements from people who have dreamt of famous movie or TV stars, with whom they never had any contact, and whom they were not very likely to ever meet. These dreams usually pair the dreamer with the celebrity, such as Elvis Presley, the Osmonds, the late Freddie Prinz, and John Travolta. Concern is expressed about the star's safety or well-being and when the dreamer wakes up, he/she is usually confused about the whole thing, sometimes even embarrassed. It is not a question of fanatical fans who daydream themselves into situations that could never occur, nor can one dismiss these dream fantasies necessarily as pure imagination. Take the case of one of my Canadian readers, Mrs. Susan P. A mother of 34 years of age, not given to flights of fancy, she nevertheless had detailed and persistent dreams about John Travolta that literally haunted her.

It started in February, 1979 with a dream in which the star, whom she had never even seen in a movie, appeared on her street and complained about a bad throat. The next dream showed Travolta wearing a beard at a time when he did not yet wear one. Still another dream showed her with the star visiting someone in a hospital. There was a male patient in one of the beds, and wires were connected to his body from some sort of apparatus. At the time, Mrs. P.'s father was very ill in the hospital, but later she discovered that Travolta's father had had a heart attack about the same time and was also hospitalized. The joint dream visit to a hospital has definite clairvoyant overtones, it would seem.

There is a strong emotional concern within Mrs. P. connecting her with the star which she cannot explain on rational grounds. She has dreamt about Travolta flying his own plane and fears for his safety in this respect. When she thinks of him, she becomes uncontrollably depressed.

This is the kind of dream you cannot explain as simple fan adulation; perhaps Mrs. P. is clairvoyant and, for some unknown reason, there is a tie between her and the star—perhaps from another lifetime?

Out-of-the-body dreams: astral travel is a common phenomenon.

Nearly everybody at one time or another has what used to be called an "astral projection" but nowadays is more commonly referred to as "out-of-the-body experience." In this phenomenon, the person rises from the physical body, and floats up toward the ceiling, then travels outside and is able to visit and observe people and situations at a distance, and to remember them clearly on awakening. Frequently, when the astral traveler returns to the physical body, there is the sensation of falling or spinning down from a great height, and on awakening, many astral travelers have complained about being "very tired"—as travelers might be!

William H. Updegrove is a piano tuner and technician, 70 years old, who has lived with the psychic all his life. While still in college, he had an out-of-the-body experience, during which he was able to observe everything that happened to him.

"I could see my body lying on the bed, but I was high in the air, connected to my body by a thin cord. I traveled in spirit to the school building where I had attended elementary school; went through the stone wall, and to the very desk that I had used many years before.This was about thirty miles that I had traveled in the astral."

Out-of-the-body experiences occur often during surgery, as a result of anesthetics being administered to the patient. A lady in California described to me in minute detail what she saw below herself on the operating table; the patient (herself) had apparently "died" clinically and the doctor frantically tried to revive her. She heard every word uttered by them as they sought to bring her back to life, and finally, with an expression of utter dejection, gave up. At that moment, the woman slipped back into her body, and, to the surprise of her surgeons, returned to life without further delay. When she later reported the conversation she had overheard while in the astral state, the surgeons did not know what to make of it, having been trained only in conventional medicine where there is as yet no place for psychic occurrences.

Her dead mother came to her in a dream.

While we are asleep, it is easiest for psychic contact to occur. At that time, the bonds between conscious mind and unconscious are loose and the very fine "radio waves" from the next stage of existence can penetrate our unconscious minds. However, it is also true that sometimes the departed can actually project themselves to us and though we experience their visits in our dreams, they are actual visits which could have taken place in the waking state as well, if we were sufficiently relaxed to perceive them.

Mrs. Ruth K. of Georgia is a very devout Christian. One morning not long ago, she "dreamt" that her late mother came to her and said, "This morning in church you will sing hymn number 467."

On awakening, Mrs. K. told her husband of the unusual dream, and then they went off to church. When Mrs. K.'s mother died, the funeral was marked by hymn singing, as she had wanted it to be. Thus, hymns meant a great deal to the departed mother.

Well, when they arrived in church, sure enough the second hymn was number 467, and it was sung by the entire congregation. Her husband looked at Mrs. K. with a strange expression, but she never told the minister about her dream. She doesn't know what made him choose number 467 that morning, but apparently her late mother knew beforehand, and used this knowledge to prove her continued existence in the world beyond.

Debra F. of Michigan had a similar though in one respect different experience. The night her beloved great-grandfather passed away, she was only nine years old, but his death hit her very hard. That night, in bed, she suddenly saw her late great-grandfather, and she knew it was him by the outline of his tall figure. A great feeling of love and peace came with it, and as he vanished again, she was at peace and had learned to accept his passing.

Final visits by people about to go on to the next phase of existence are very common, especially when the fact of continuing life beyond the veil came as a surprise to them, or to their families.

The Devil attacked her friend in a bizarre dream.

N.O. of California had a bizarre dream in which the Devil attacked one of her friends. "He's got hoofs like a deer, and burnt red skin, no clothes, very hairy, a tail and horns on his head," she writes.

"He has a sickle in his hand and is holding the girl over the railing of the stairs and he makes one big slash in her chest.

"I cannot relate this dream to my life at all. I am 26 years old and single. I live with my parents and am out of work."

The key lies in the last two sentences. N.O.'s unconscious is trying to tell her that if she behaved like "the Devil," perhaps she would be neither single nor out of work. The dream is essentially caused by her dissatisfaction with the current state of her life.

Dreaming of a former life.

Once in a while a recurrent dream indicates memories of a former lifetime, reincarnation, though this is the exception rather than the rule. Only when a dream recurs persistently and always in the same way, does it indicate such a solution.

Among the thousands of recurrent dreams I have examined, none was more startling than the dream brought to my attention by a young hospital worker in Illinois, Pamela Wollenberg, who could not understand why she kept hearing a young woman give her the cryptic message of "Scotland 1600-Ruthveen-Gowrie-I leapt." As she had never been to Scotland and had no Anglo-Saxon background, nor had read anything dealing with Scotland at that period, the whole question of this repeated dream became a puzzle. Then one day I found an obscure, locally printed booklet in a Scottish manor house, in which the story of Huntingtower Castle was revealed. It appeared that the dream referred to the Ruthveen family, whose first-born son was always called Lord Gowrie. In the year 1600, the last two Gowries (or Ruthveens) were executed by King's orders on trumped up charges of treason, the so-called

"Gowrie Conspiracy," and Gowrie Castle later became Huntingtower Castle; the Gowries were to disappear from the records of history by Royal decree.

One of the young women of the clan had escaped from her lover's room by jumping (leaping) over the roof from one tower to the other. Apparently, a later Lady Gowrie tried to emulate that feat, but failed and fell to her death. It was she who somehow incarnated again in the young hospital worker from upstate Illinois!

What had started as a recurrent dream was later researched by me through hypnotic regression, and much more evidential information came from the lips of a young girl who could not possibly have known, or had access to this knowledge. Recurrent dreams with reincarnation meaning happen only in cases where a life has been terminated abruptly or prematurely in some fashion, like a bonus of knowledge in the next life, if only in the dream state.

Amazing "haunting" by healing spirit.

There are dreams that aren't really dreams. Instead, they are in-between states where the person is partially awake and real events take place rather than imaginary ones.

For instance, A.P. of New York writes, "In my dream, I was cold and hungry. I woke up, or thought I woke up.

"All of a sudden, I heard someone at my door. I couldn't move at all. I felt a strong presence of a being. The being walked through my room and stopped at my bed.

"I tried to scream or run out but I felt a magnetic power holding me still. I could tell the being was male and very large. He held his right hand over my chest, passing his hands over my body from my head to my waist.

"Then he walked out and was gone. As soon as he left, my eyes opened and my chest was hot. I was scared and shaking."

From this description, I think it likely that A.P. had a partial out-of-the-body experience—that is why she could not move or open her eyes.

The visitor need not have scared her. I feel this was a spirit entity who had come to give her a healing.

J.M. of South Carolina writes, "I dreamed of being in a white frame house. Looking out the window, I saw a black hearse driving slowly up.

"A knock at the door sounded and upon opening it, I was surprised to see my deceased father standing there, seemingly oblivious of my presence. He walked into the room and immediately fell to the floor. Three shrill 'swoosh' type sounds preceded the fall, and my dad seemed to vanish."

The return of the father's spirit in what is meant to convey death—the hearse—serves as an ominous warning. The three sounds may connect with a time element such as three weeks or months. J.M. should hope for the best, but be prepared in case tragedy does strike.

When a dream is not a dream.

Sometimes people experience what they think is a dream, but which in reality is a psychic experience occurring when they awake. Because so many of these events happen at night, and because they are often hard to accept on a rational, everyday basis, people prefer to explain them as dreams rather than reality.

A case in point was reported to me by Ingrid F., who is married to a soldier and lives with him on the base in Texas. About four weeks ago she was asleep, when around midnight she opened her eyes and to her surprise saw a ghostly figure standing in the bedroom. Although she could not make out a face, she had the distinct feeling the figure was staring at her. Her first thought was that perhaps a burglar had gotten into the house. Then it occurred to her it might be her husband, trying to play a prank on her, but a quick glance over to his bed showed him to be fast asleep.

Far from being afraid, Ingrid F. decided to question the apparition about its intentions, and at that moment she recognized it as being female, wearing a dress that seemed vaguely familiar to her. She recalled later that she had seen such a dress some years ago in the basement of her mother's house in Germany. But before she could question the ghostly figure, the visitor turned around and walked into the door, disappearing instantly.

For a long time afterward, Ingrid F. was unsure whether she had dreamt the whole incident, but on further recollection she was equally sure that she had not. The visitor has not returned since, and Ingrid still wonders who it might have been, and why she had come to her that night.

Judging from the clothes Ingrid F. recognized, the visitor might have been a relative of hers from Europe, concerned with something happening in Ingrid's personal life. Not a ghost in the true sense but a free spirit, she might have come to warn, or cause Ingrid to think of life beyond. At any rate, though spirits can communicate easiest in the dream state, when the bonds between conscious and unconscious are loose, this was definitely not a dream, rather a waking experience at the boundaries of sleep.

HOW DREAMS
CAN IMPROVE
YOUR LIFE

Inasmuch as being asleep is the same as dreaming, as I have pointed out earlier in this book, the sleep-dream state can be used successfully to enhance knowledge and the ability to learn. This need not be done through hypnosis undertaken by a professional hypnotist, although that too is possible. It can be done with reasonable expectancy of success by the dreamer him/herself. The principle underlying such self help is that of the "soft sell" of the unconscious, in a way which allows the unconscious to absorb the suggestions given without rejecting them, as it might if concentration or "hard sell" methods were to be used. For that reason, all mechanical gadgets, such as recordings played all night at a low level in order to penetrate the unconscious, have proven to be spectacularly unsuccessful. The only way in which the unconscious can be made to serve the master in the waking condition is through the dream state in a soft, off hand condition, as if it didn't really matter whether the suggestion were to be adopted or not. This approach I have found to be highly successful in most cases, based upon experience and observation, and without really knowing why it is easier to streamline the unconscious into working for the conscious mind in this seemingly weak manner rather than in a formally organized, aggressive approach. Perhaps it has to do with a built-in resistance on the part of the unconscious to take orders when they are patently packaged as firm orders, while succumbing to slight suggestions, especially when they do not seem to be pressed but offered merely as possibilities. The unconscious mind has a sort of life of its own, and I have found it to be a petulant child rather than a reasoning adult.

What I am suggesting is nothing less than programming your dreams, in that certain simple ideas are being agreed upon prior to going to sleep, then fed to the unconscious in the hope that the digestion by the dream state will result in acquiring knowledge on the conscious level which can be utilized in the wakeful state. That this is not always fully successful can well be understood, considering that dream material from various sources also competes for the time period during sleep when this process should be completed. Since it is impossible to turn off the external or even the internal input of dream material into the sleeper during the night, one can only hope that some of the program material will find its own place, perhaps superseding some of the other material, perhaps waiting for an opening when it can slip into the unconscious. Be this as it may, the attempt can be successful, and if not at first, should be repeated until it is. Here then are the instructions on how to proceed:

1. Between thirty and sixty minutes prior to desired sleeping time, withdraw to a quiet place, where you can rest with subdued light. You should be alone, so as not to be embarrassed when you vocalize certain commands. At this point, read the desired information, once silently and once vocally. This may be anything from a paragraph to a full book, of course, but chances are that you will succeed best with a few pages at a time. Having thus committed the information to the upper levels of your conscious mind, but by no means remembered them, you put away the source material and immediately change your mind, change to a subject totally different from what you have just read and in no way connected with it. This should preferably be a pleasant subject, allowing you to imagine yourself being involved in it in some fashion.

2. Prior to sleeping time, look at the material once again without reading it, merely taking in a visual image of the pages you wish to commit to your memory. End this by saying "This I shall remember on awakening," then again change the subject of your thoughts and don't dwell on the matter at hand.

3. The following morning have another look at the material, again without reading it and you will discover that much, if not all, of it has already been committed to memory, *while you slept*.

Not only material to be learned can thus be integrated into the unconscious and from there into the conscious mind, but questions that you could not answer the night before may very well find answers the following day, after you have put the question to the unconscious prior to retiring. There is really no limit to the way in which the dream process can be put to use to digest and process the material in question. In a sense, it acts like a human computer, taking the material put into it and producing answers that you were unable to arrive at on a purely logical, conscious level.

If there are dreams which leave you puzzled, even after you have consulted the list of categories I have offered in this work, and you wish to have additional, perhaps more detailed information on the subject of your dream, it is possible to go back to the source another night. Simply suggest to your unconscious that you will find elaboration of the previous dream. In order to do this, recap in your mind what you remember of the puzzling dream, then ask the question, both mentally and vocally prior to retiring. Chances are you may dream the same dream, or perhaps the same dream advanced slightly, and may find answers that have escaped you on the previous occasion.

Although a great deal of material received in the dream state is put into us from external sources, much of it derives from our own selves, from levels of consciousness we seldom use. Dreams are merely states of consciousness, they are not entities unto themselves, they are not a single category of condition: my purpose in discussing the many facets of dream usage is to acquaint my readers with the true nature of the dream state, and its many promises. The ultimate goal is to discipline one's dream perception to the point where much if not all of the dream material is remembered upon arising, and where the dream channel can be opened so wide that it serves as a secondary world of perception, equal or perhaps superior to the state of wakefulness which so many consider as the major portion of our existence. In actuality, wakefulness and the dream state go hand in hand, and are equal partners in our day to day existence, sharing consciousness, and forming the two halves of our lives.

BIBLIOGRAPHY

Bro, Harmon H. *Dreams in the Life of Prayer*. New York: Harper, 1970.

_____. *Edgar Cayce on Dreams*. New York: Paperback Lib., 1974.

Chetwynd, Tom. *How to Interpret Your Own Dreams*. New York: Wyden, 1972.

Faraday, Ann. *The Dream Game*. New York: Harper, 1974.

Fromm, Erich. *The Forgotten Language*. New York: Harper, 1951.

Hall, Calvin S. *The Meaning of Dreams*. New York: McGraw, 1966.

Linde, Shirley Motter, and Savery, Louis M. *The Sleep Book*. New York: Harper, 1974.

MacKenzie, Norman. *Dreams and Dreaming*. New York: Vanguard, 1965.

Monroe, Robert A. *Journeys Out of the Body*. Garden City, New York: Doubleday, 1971; Anchor, 1973.

Muldoon, Sylvan and Hereward Carrington. *Phenomena of Astral Projection*. New York: Weiser, 1970.

_____. *Projection of Astral Body*. New York: Weiser, 1970.

Sabin, Katharine Cover. *ESP and Dream Analysis*. Chicago: Regnery, 1974.

Shulman, Sandra. *Dreams*. New York: Harrow Books, 1973.

STAY IN TOUCH

On the following pages you will find some of the books now available on related subjects. Your book dealer stocks most of these and will stock new titles in the Llewellyn series as they become available. We urge your patronage.

To obtain our full catalog write for our bimonthly news magazine/catalog, *Llewellyn's New Worlds of Mind and Spirit*. A sample copy is free, and it will continue coming to you at no cost as long as you are an active mail customer. Or you may subscribe for just $10.00 in the U.S.A. and Canada ($20.00 overseas, first class mail). Many bookstores also have *New Worlds* available to their customers. Ask for it.

Llewellyn's New Worlds of Mind and Spirit
**P.O. Box 64383-369, St. Paul, MN 55164-0383,
U.S.A.**

TO ORDER BOOKS AND TAPES

If your book dealer does not have the books described, you may order them directly from the publisher by sending full price in U.S. funds, plus $3.00 for postage and handling for orders *under* $10.00; $4.00 for orders *over* $10.00. There are no postage and handling charges for orders over $50.00. Postage and handling rates are subject to change. We ship UPS whenever possible. Delivery guaranteed. Provide your street address as UPS does not deliver to P.O. Boxes. UPS to Canada requires a $50.00 minimum order. Allow 4-6 weeks for delivery. Orders outside the U.S.A. and Canada: Airmail—add retail price of book; add $5.00 for each non-book item (tapes, etc.); add $1.00 per item for surface mail. Mail orders to:

**LLEWELLYN PUBLICATIONS
P.O. Box 64383-369, St. Paul, MN 55164-0383,
U.S.A.**

ESP, WITCHES & UFOS:
The Best of Hans Holzer, Book II
Edited by Ray Buckland

In this exciting anthology, best-selling author and psychic investigator Hans Holzer explores true accounts of the strange and unknown: telepathy, psychic and reincarnation dreams, survival after death, psycho-ecstasy, unorthodox healings, Pagans and Witches, and Ufonauts. Reports included in this volume:

• Mrs. F. dreamed of a group of killers and was particularly frightened by the eyes of their leader. Ten days later, the Sharon Tate murders broke into the headlines. When Mrs. F. saw the photo of Charles Manson, she immediately recognized him as the man from her dream.

• How you can use four simple "wish-fulfillment" steps to achieve psycho-ecstasy—turning a negative situation into something positive.

• Several true accounts of miraculous healings achieved by unorthodox medical practitioners.

• How the author, when late to meet with a friend and unable to find a telephone nearby, sent a telepathic message to his friend via his friend's answering service.

• The reasons why more and more people are turning to Witchcraft and Paganism as a way of life.

• When UFOs land—physical evidence vs. cultists.

These reports and many more will entertain and enlighten all readers intrigued by the mysteries of life ... and beyond!

0-87542-368-X, 304 pgs., mass market $4.95